Returning God's Call

By John C. Purdy

Returning God's Call: The Challenge of Christian Living

Parables at Work

Edited by John C. Purdy

Always Being Reformed: The Future of Church Education

Returning God's Call

The Challenge of Christian Living

John C. Purdy

Westminster/John Knox Press
Louisville, Kentucky

Scripture quotations are from the Revised Standard Version of the Bible, copyrighted 1946, 1952, © 1971, 1973 by the Division of Christian Education of the National Council of the Churches of Christ in the U.S.A., and are used by permission.

The poem by Elmer F. Suderman in chapter 2 appeared in *Theology Today,* April 1971, under the title "The Smell of Perfumed Assemblies," and is used by permission of the author and the publisher.

Book design by Gene Harris

First edition

Published by Westminster/John Knox Press
Louisville, Kentucky

PRINTED IN THE UNITED STATES OF AMERICA

9 8 7 6 5 4 3 2

Library of Congress Cataloging-in-Publication Data

Purdy, John C. (John Clifford), 1925–
    Returning God's call : the challenge of Christian living / John C. Purdy. — 1st ed.
        p.   cm.
    Includes index.
    ISBN 0-664-25046-7 (pbk.)

    1. Christian life—Biblical teaching. 2. Bible.
N.T. Matthew—Criticism, interpretation, etc. I. Title.
BS2545.C48P87 1989
248.4—dc19   88–26153
                                                                      CIP

Contents

1

Hearers of the Call

Paul, called by the will of God to be an apostle of Jesus Christ . . . to the church of God . . . to those sanctified in Christ Jesus, called to be saints together with all those who in every place call on the name of our Lord Jesus Christ, both their Lord and ours. . . . God is faithful, by whom you were called into the fellowship of his Son, Jesus Christ our Lord . . . consider your call.
—1 Corinthians 1:1–2, 9, 26a

What metaphor of the Christian life have you chosen? We act out the images we have of ourselves. The way we see ourselves as Christians determines how we behave. A picture is not only worth a thousand words, it is the parent of a thousand deeds. Do you see yourself a soldier in God's army? A sister or a brother in faith's extended family? A scholar in the school of Christ? A traveler along the Christian way? Each of these metaphors has served Christians well. William Booth, founder of the Salvation Army, used the military metaphor with great effect; slum dwellers of nineteenth-century London found the discipline of a soldier to be strong armor against the pull of a former life. The ex-soldier Ignatius Loyola, founder of the Jesuits, modeled his society after military ideas. There are Latin American priests who see themselves as chaplains to God's guerrilla army of liberation.

The idea of the Christian fellowship as a heavenly family housed on earth has a long history. The Shakers saw one another as brothers and sisters in a surrogate family; no wonder they were able so easily to adopt orphans into their communities. Roman Catholics call their priest Father; in their religious orders are Brothers and Sisters.

Life in Scottish Presbyterian parishes of a previous generation was very much like being in school: The pastor was teacher in residence; sermons were long and scholarly; when the pastor visited a home, he tested the children's knowledge of the church catechism. Andrew Murray, a Scottish-trained missionary, named his devotional classic *With Christ in the School of Prayer.*

In *Pilgrim's Progress,* John Bunyan captured the imaginations of many generations with his image of the Christian life as a journey. In his contemporary novel *The Blue Mountains of China,* Rudy Wiebe tells the story of Mennonites who moved from Germany to Russia, China, Canada, and South America—modern pilgrims in search of religious freedom. One of Wiebe's characters says, "You know the trouble with the Mennonites? They've always wanted to be Jews. To have land God had given them for their very own, to which they were called; so even if someone chased them away, they could work forever to get it back."

The New Testament is not limited to the images

of soldier, sibling, scholar, or sojourner. It offers such metaphors of the Christian life as "ambassador for Christ"—a favorite of evangelicals—and "citizen of God's commonwealth," a favorite of social activists. Then there is the disciple, the member of Christ's body, the friend of Jesus.

It is the argument of this book, however, that these various metaphors are not as useful for our time as still another: hearers of the call. If we had to select one and only one way of picturing the life of the Christian, it would be the image of one who has heard and keeps hearing a persistent summons to belief and action.

When I was a child, playing hide-and-seek outside in the waning daylight of a summer evening, inevitably our front door would open and my mother's voice would call, "Jack, time to come in!" I would go on with hide-and-seek as though nothing had happened. To anybody passing by, I looked no different from my playmates. But I *was* different; I had been "called in"; everything was changed. In a similar way Christians—who may appear no different from others—have ringing in their ears God's summons to believe and to obey. Henry Thoreau said that some march to a different drummer. Christians do not hear a different drumbeat; they hear Jesus' distant but clear voice saying, "Come, follow me." It sounds over the whir of the lathe, the cry of a baby, the clink of coins, the curses of enemies, the whisper of success, the roar of the crowd, the nagging of conscience.

An Active Voice

You may object that the metaphor of hearers of the call is too passive, too quiescent. You remember the injunction of the Letter of James: "Be doers of the word, and not hearers only." But in scripture God's call is a powerful spur to action. Moses heard the voice of God in a smoking bush and went off to lead a people out of slavery. Amos left his sycamore trees at the summons of God. We assume that Jesus himself was called to his ministry.

In *The Blue Mountains of China,* Wiebe tells the story of a Mennonite farmer named Sam Reimer. One night Sam hears a voice saying to him, "Samuel, Samuel . . . I am the God of your fathers, the Lord your God. Go and proclaim peace in Vietnam." In perplexity, Sam goes to his pastor, who tells him to listen for the voice a second time. The next night the call comes again, but Sam cannot get anyone to believe that he has truly heard God's voice. His pastor won't believe it; neither will his wife or his fellow Mennonites. The Canadian government won't give him a visa to Vietnam; the inter-Mennonite Church Service Society won't help him. Sam's reaction to these rebuffs is to give up hope and die. On his deathbed he says to his wife, "When I heard the voice, I should of gone. Left a note and gone. When you know like that, are chosen, you shouldn't wait, talk. Go."

Fritz Graebe was a civil engineer with the German army in World War II. He said that after witnessing the mass murder of Jewish civilians in the Ukrainian town of Dubno, he heard his mother's voice, saying, "And Fritz, what would you do?" He was not disobedient to that inner call. Fritz Graebe contrived to save the lives of hundreds of Jews.

The prophet Jeremiah tells the inner pain of not obeying the call of God:

> If I say, "I will not mention him,
>   or speak any more in his name,"
> there is in my heart as it were a burning fire
>   shut up in my bones,
> and I am weary with holding it in,
>   and I cannot.
>
> —Jeremiah 20:9

Right for Our Times

What is so timely about the metaphor of hearers of the call? It has several considerable advantages. First, as we shall demonstrate, it is an extraordinarily rich metaphor; it is applicable to a whole range of settings—family, piety, economics, missions, stewardship, enmities, caring ministries, marriage. No other single biblical metaphor has such range. The soldier metaphor is fine for warring against injustice, but "Onward, Christian Soldiers" is not to be hummed when you sit down with your spouse to discuss household finances. Family metaphors don't help with civic responsibilities. The scholar metaphor is useful for worship and Bible study, but books like Andrew Murray's *With Christ in the School of Prayer* don't have much to say about faithfulness in the workplace. The sojourner metaphor, too, is hard to reconcile with domestic responsibilities.

Hearers of the call also puts us in direct line

with Abraham, Moses, David, the prophets, and
the apostles, all of whom have this in common:
They were summoned by God to fulfill the divine
purpose.

Hearers of the call has a particular resonance in
our culture, dominated as it is by the mass media.
All of us are audiences for television, computer
networks, radio, and publishing. We are constantly being studied (by researchers) and wooed
(by advertisers and politicos) through the mass
media. We live in a world that increasingly orga-
nizes us into audiences and wants to deal with us
as audiences. Russell Baker, writing in the *New
York Times* (September 30, 1987), said, "Since
1952, the electorate has been treated by politi-
cians less and less as an electorate and more and
more as an audience." If we are indeed treated
more and more as audience, one of the primary
ethical tasks of our time is to sort out the various
appeals to our ears.

The metaphor of hearers of the call has one
additional advantage, which will be referred to in
more detail in chapter 11: It applies to the church
as a collective as well as to the individual Christian. One of the considerable threats to the health
and welfare of Christianity in our generation is a
tendency to individualism. Carl Dudley character-
izes the religious attitude of many young adults as
"believing but not belonging." This is American
individualism at its most typical. If we are to over-
come the tendency of our age to privatism, we
need metaphors that suggest collective as well as
individual obedience and commitment.

We shall test the usefulness of hearers of the
call by examining ten "calling" narratives from

the Gospel of Matthew. This Gospel is particularly useful for our purpose, for it contains a number of accounts in which Jesus is represented as issuing summonses to various persons: calling fishermen to leave their nets; calling those same fishermen to take up the cross, follow a life of humble service, and go into the world with the good news of the kingdom. Some scholars say that Matthew was written as a Christian handbook, a manual of discipline. If so, that makes it particularly useful as a source for examining various calls to discipleship.

Another feature of Matthew invites the attention of those who want to invest discipleship with new meaning: The Gospel is structured of five large chunks of Jesus' teaching, each preceded by narrative. John Meier calls these five discourses "the five pillars of the Gospel." The author of Matthew was most likely a Jewish Christian leader of the church in Syria in the late first century A.D., writing at a time when the church had split from the Jewish synagogue and was struggling to define itself. The five pillars and their accompanying narratives suggest that the Gospel writer saw Jesus as a new Moses: As Moses called Israel to leave Egypt and go adventuring in the wilderness, where he delivered to them the commandments of God, so Jesus calls the church to a new obedience, "to boldly go where no one has gone before," in the famous words from *Star Trek*.

In keeping with the notion that hearers of the call is a collective metaphor, we shall invite to the discussion four authors of popular commentaries on the First Gospel: Jack Dean Kingsbury, an American Protestant and author of *Matthew* in

Proclamation Commentaries (Fortress Press, 1986); David Hill, a Britisher, author of *The Gospel of Matthew* in the New Century Bible Commentary (Wm. B. Eerdmans Publishing Co., 1972); John P. Meier, an American Roman Catholic, author of *Matthew* in the New Testament Message Series (Michael Glazier, 1980): and Eduard Schweizer, a Swiss, author of *The Good News According to Matthew* translated by David Green (John Knox, 1975). Quotations from these four books will be indicated by the author's name and the page reference in parenthesis.

Christ as God's Call

One further consideration remains, before we look at specific narratives in Matthew. What particular force or import are we to assign to a call from Jesus Christ? Is a call something like a sermon, in which we are exhorted to a new kind of behavior? Is the listing of ten calls from Jesus an attempt to replace the Ten Commandments with a new table of moral requirements? Is a call something like an invitation to join a party, which we may accept or refuse depending on our mood?

The answer lies in the identity of the one who issues the call. There are various ways in which the identity of Jesus in Matthew's Gospel is described. Some see Jesus presented as the divine Son of God (Kingsbury). Others see him presented to the reader as the Son of man, who will return at the end of time to judge everyone for his or her deeds (Meier). Some see Matthew's Jesus as "Messiah and Son of Man and supremely Lord of the Church" (Hill, p. 43).

As Hans Frei points out in a series of essays in *Crossroads,* a person's identity is revealed in what he does, how he enacts his intentions. The Jesus we see in Matthew's Gospel is the person who is perfectly obedient to the will of God, so that the one who calls us is the one who himself hears and truly obeys the Father's will. His verbal summons is at one with the example of his life. He is the one of whom the apostle Paul wrote, "Have this mind among yourselves, which is yours in Christ Jesus, who, though he was in the form of God, did not count equality with God a thing to be grasped, but emptied himself, taking the form of a servant, being born in the likeness of men. And being found in human form he humbled himself and became obedient unto death, even death on a cross" (Phil. 2:5–8).

In Jesus, the call of God comes to us in two ways: in the example of his own obedience, through which the world is saved from sin; and through his verbal calls. We may say then in answer to the question, Who is this Jesus who calls to us from the pages of scripture? that he is the one who in both deed and word summons us to fulfill our Creator's intent.

2

The Call to Adventure

From that time Jesus began to preach, saying, "Repent, for the kingdom of heaven is at hand."

As he walked by the Sea of Galilee, he saw two brothers, Simon who is called Peter and Andrew his brother, casting a net into the sea; for they were fishermen. And he said to them, "Follow me, and I will make you fishers of men." Immediately they left their nets and followed him. And going on from there he saw two other brothers, James the son of Zebedee and John his brother, in the boat with Zebedee their father, mending their nets, and he called them. Immediately they left the boat and their father, and followed him.

—Matthew 4:17–22

Christianity began as a workingman's religion. No, that is not the gospel according to Marx; it is the Gospel According to Matthew. Matthew tells us that immediately after Jesus began a public preaching ministry, he took four fishermen as his apprentices. He was walking by the Sea of Galilee and spied Andrew and Peter casting their nets. He called them to follow him, promising to make them fishers of men. In Matthew's Gospel, then,

linked tightly together are Jesus' ringing pronouncement, "Repent, for the kingdom of heaven
is at hand," and his invitation to the fishermen,
"Follow me."

Matthew's narrative wastes no time in describing how the new movement grew: Brothers Peter
and Andrew left their nets to go with Jesus. And
as the three were going along the shore together,
they came upon three other fishermen—Zebedee
and his two sons, James and John. Jesus called the
two brothers also; they left their father in the boat
and went with Jesus and the others. A carpenter's
son and four fishermen—that was the beginning
of the Christian church, as Matthew tells the
story. Quite literally, the church began as a workingman's movement.

And where the church has prospered it has, in
some measure, remained a workingman and
workingwoman's movement. It has kept tightly
linked Jesus' pronouncement of the impending
kingdom of God and the call to working people to
follow him who inaugurates that kingdom.

That should not be interpreted as a partisan
political statement. Long before critics invented
the sociological concept of the working class there
were two kinds of people in the world, those who
worked for a living and those who did not. The
Christian church has always done better among
those who have worked for a living. When it has
catered to men and women of leisure, it has gone
to seed. And, like winged dandelion seed, it has
been carried about by shifting winds of change,
following now this fad, now that. For what have
people of leisure to do but seek the latest fancy?
The fate of the church that forgets its working-

class roots was never better described than in this
poem by Elmer F. Suderman:

> Here they come,
> my nonchalants,
> my lazy daisies,
> their dainty perfume
> disturbing the room
> the succulent smell
> seductive as hell.
>
> Here they are,
> my pampered flamboyants,
> status spoiled, who bring
> with exquisite zing
> their souls spick and span
> protected by Ban,
> their hearts young and gay
> decked in handsome cliché,
> exchanging at my call
> with no effort at all
> worship for whispering,
> God for gossiping,
> theology for television.
>
> Baptized in the smell
> of classic Chanel
> I promote their nod
> to a jaunty God
> Who, they are sure,
> is a sparkling gem
> superbly right for them.
>
> There they go,
> my in-crowd,
> my soft-skinned crowd,
> my sun-tanned, so-so

> elegant, swellegant,
> natty, delectable,
> suave, cool, adorable
> DAMNED!

Wherever the church allows "the kingdom of heaven is at hand" to be separated from Jesus' call to working people to follow him, the game is up. The vital nerve of the Christian movement has been severed. The positive proof of this negative judgment is the enormous appeal of Methodism to the English working classes of the eighteenth century. An Anglican church that had become the private club of landed and titled people had run out of energy. When the Wesleyans went with the gospel to working men and women, the church in England experienced a great revival.

The affinity of the gospel and of the working class lies in this: Any religion that does not get at the working core of persons will not have much hold on them. For a religion to succeed, it must in some way claim the working hours of its adherents. It must win what Wayne Oates aptly calls "the vocational heart of the person's being." Some religions, it is true, succeed precisely by helping persons forget the misery and drudgery of daily toil; but such faiths provide a means for coping with work, they do not ignore it.

It has been the particular genius of Christianity never to forget that it began as a working-man's religion. Enormous vitality has flowed from the coupling of daily work to faith in a better future. Ann Lee, who founded the movement known as Shakers, said of her conversion, "I gave my heart to God and my hands to work."

From the belief of the Shakers that every daily
chore was a service done unto God flowed their
superb craftsmanship.

Therefore, just as it is important for Americans
to face backward and to take their bearings from
the Declaration of Independence, so Christians
need from time to time to examine their charter.
The account of the Calling of the Fishermen,
standing at the very beginning of Jesus' ministry,
serves as a charter for the Christian movement.
Two things in particular need to be recalled about
that narrative.

Work and Religion

*Jesus' call to the four Galileans served to make
neither a religion of work nor a work of religion.*
He said to them neither "Follow me, and I will
make you better fishermen" nor "Follow me, and
never again will you have to fish for a living."
Jesus' call should not be interpreted to mean either that work has henceforth a sacred quality to
it or that being a follower of Jesus is a full-time
occupation that replaces the necessity to work as
others do.

Some would make of the Calling of the Four a
holy baptism of daily work; they would use it to
mark work as sacred to Christ. Jesus called four
callus-handed fishermen to be his disciples, goes
the argument; therefore, work is what fits persons
for the kingdom of God. Jesus came to the workplace to find disciples; those who are in the workplace stand on hallowed ground. True, there have
been times in Christendom when an occupation
was regarded as one's high and holy calling from

God, and this account of the calling of the fishermen was used to justify that view. Housewives
cooked and cleaned to the glory of God; farmers
plowed to the glory of God. In effect, Jesus' call
made a religion of work.

However, more often the opposite interpretation of Matthew 4:18–22 is given: All who would be
truly Christian must forsake ordinary employ-
ment and become full-time workers for the Lord.
Their total time and energy is to be given to making converts for the faith. Appeals to young people
to enlist in church occupations—which are described as full-time Christian service—are based
on this same text. In this view, religion becomes
work. The pursuit of religious faith for oneself and
of converts for the movement is regarded as the
highest understanding of work.

While both notions of the proper relationship of
faith and work have some validity, the story of the
Call of the Fishermen cannot be used to support
either view. The effect of Jesus' call was not to
make Andrew, Peter, James, and John full-time
Christian workers, nor was it to make daily work
a sacrament. Look again at the narrative.

Jesus appears by the sea and calls to four young
men to follow him. Andrew and Peter respond by
abandoning—for the moment—the tools of their
trade. "They left their nets and followed him."
The other two brothers run off and leave their
father to manage the family fishing business all by
himself. There is no way to read this narrative as
a glorification of work! If anything, the story
teaches quite the opposite. It shows five young
Galileans, under the banner of God's kingdom,
going off on a lark, leaving the older folks to do

their chores. Shades of Tom Sawyer and Huck Finn!

But if the story cannot be used to make a religion of work, neither ought it be used to make a work of religion. "Fishers of men" clearly implies some kind of task. It is not simply to be with Jesus and enjoy his company that the four are summoned. There is a purpose in their calling; there is work to be done; there is a goal, which will require as much or more energy than hauling nets and cleaning fish.

But if the narrative serves to make neither a religion of work nor a work of religion, what is its effect? Matthew 4:17–22 gently pries apart work and faith so that work can be seen for what it is: a part of God's creation but nothing sacred in and of itself. The narrative serves as a gentle reproof of two popular misunderstandings: (1) that the life of faith is all work and no play, and (2) that work is faith in action. However popular these notions may be, both are heretical. Neither represents the biblical understanding of our work and God's work.

God's Work and Ours

According to scripture, work is an essential and necessary part of human life—no more, no less. Let us say once more, for emphasis, what we have already said about the Call of the Fishermen: *Jesus' summons to a life of faith and obedience desacralizes work.* It was the fishermen, not their boats and nets, that Jesus wanted. Those things are holy that are set apart for special use by the

Deity. In this particular narrative the fishermen alone were set apart for God's special use.

It may be said of the four that once they had followed the trade of fishing, but no more. Henceforth they followed Jesus. You and I, who believe in Jesus Christ and count ourselves his disciples, are not to follow a trade or profession as though it were the Holy Grail. We are to follow Jesus. Work is to take a secondary role in our lives. If Christ is truly our Master, then work cannot be equally important. We may be engaged in work, but never married to it. And whenever we are pressed or tempted to make work supreme, we are to recall the story of the four fishermen. We are to remember how they left their nets and their boats to go and be with Jesus, to do what he would have them do.

If work is not to command all our time and energy and devotion, what is left? Work is part of God's ordering of creation; it belongs to our humanity that we work. To be a human being is to work. It is that simple—and that profound. In the second chapter of Genesis it says that after God created the garden, the human was put in it to tend it and till it. In the very beginning of things human beings are pictured as stewards of creation. The first human being was an ecologist. Even before Adam became a husband, he was a husbandman. Not a creature with no responsibilities and no tasks, like the other animals, but one put on earth as in a lovely garden, to care for it.

In the next chapter of Genesis we hear the story of the fall. Adam and Eve were not content with caring for God's garden, they hankered for a man-

agerial role. And so the idyll was spoiled. But
while through sin the good order of God's creation
was marred, it was not erased. Work became for
humanity a drudgery—almost a curse. Yet work
still belongs to the order of creation. As Robert
Calhoun said many years ago in *God and the Day's
Work,* "Man is by nature—and not by choice—a
worker . . . man, then, is a working animal." Work
is the divine calling given to all of humanity. That
is how it has been from the very beginning. Even
the fall has not erased that.

That reality seems to underlie Jesus' choice of
four workingmen to begin his movement. He did
not choose his first disciples from the priestly class
or from the leisure class. Nor were they intellectu-
als, academics, poets, professional athletes, or the
unemployed young. Jesus chose four fishermen.
He began his own work by coming to us in our
most natural state, while we were at work. When
the fishermen first heard Jesus' invitation to discipleship, they smelled of tar and fish. True, Jesus
called them to set aside, for a time, their fishing
gear. That is a clear signal that daily work is not
a divine mandate, as though God had set us all to
work and we dare not rest so long as we have
strength and daylight. However, Jesus *did* come
to men while they were at work. This is a strong
affirmation of the role of work in human life.

No Specific Content

Note this also about Jesus' call to the fishermen:
It had no specific content. He said simply, "Follow
me, and I will make you fishers of men." The summons is cryptic. Commentators like David Hill do

not think so. "This image [fishers of men] indicates that the disciples will be preachers and active witnesses of the Kingdom: they will be as effective in seeking men as they have been in catching fish" (p. 106). But that kind of interpretation requires that we read the Gospel backwards, that we already know about the sending of the disciples out into the world to extend Jesus' ministry. In this initial contact between Jesus and the disciples in Matthew's narrative, "fishers of men" might mean almost anything. It is a metaphor with no obvious point of reference. In what sense were the four to fish for men? Jesus did not tell them. It belongs to the nature of Jesus' call that the fishermen were to come after him without knowing precisely what they were to be or do! It is not until the final paragraph of Matthew's Gospel that it becomes fully clear what "fishers of men" means. There it is that Jesus gives to his disciples the Great Commission: They are to go into all the world and make disciples of the nations.

That end, however, is not visible from the beginning. All that Andrew, Peter, John, and James can hear is "Follow me." They go after Jesus with little knowledge of what it is they have signed on to do. They are like soldiers who have enlisted in an army to fight in a war yet to be declared; like actors who have signed up to perform roles in a play that is still being written. Jesus' call to them is a summons to step out into the unknown; it is a call to adventure.

Brother Lawrence was an ex-soldier in the Middle Ages who joined himself to a monastic order. He was put in charge of the kitchen. For reasons of his own, he resolved to practice the presence of

God in his kitchen. In whatever he did—scrubbing pots, shelling peas, mopping floors—he worked as though God were there. His efforts are recorded in a set of letters to friends and colleagues, letters later printed in a book that has become a devotional classic, *The Practice of the Presence of God.* This ex-soldier did not want to write a devotional classic; he did not intend anything designed to make him saintly or famous. He set out on an uncommon adventure in the most mundane of settings, though he would not himself have called it an adventure. If asked about it, he probably would have shrugged and said that he felt called to do it.

If there is one person living in our own lifetime who is apt to be remembered as a saint, it is Mother Teresa of Calcutta, who has devoted herself to the destitute and dying of India. Although she has appeared on national TV and has walked and talked with presidents and popes, certainly she did not set out to become world-famous. Rather, she had a modest but unflinching desire to help people; she had a call, if you please. Any Roman Catholic nun might have used her office to do what Teresa did, but she found an extraordinary way to use an ordinary office.

Surely William Shakespeare did not set out to write great literature, nor Handel to write classical music; nor did the mother of John and Charles Wesley, when she spanked them for mischief, say to herself, "I am training up the leaders of Methodism." When Abe Lincoln first ran for public office in Illinois, surely it was not with the ambition of being the Great Emancipator. Our conventional thinking is backwards. We suppose that persons once decided to be great and influential, rather than remain mired in the ordinary. It is just the opposite. They found in the ordinary workplace an occasion for doing what they would have described as their duty or their calling.

It is dangerous to pile up examples of persons who have made of an ordinary place or a run-of-the-mill office an opportunity for extraordinary service to God and to humanity. That would serve to make heroic what is commonplace. For the call of Jesus to all Christians is to make the workplace the scene of obedience, with no blueprint given of just what that obedience might look like. As with the Gospel of Matthew, it is only in retrospect that we can say that our occupations were great commissions. We are simply to allow the workplace to be an occasion for Jesus' call to faithful service. In commenting on the story of Jesus and the Fishermen, Eduard Schweizer certainly got it right when he observed (p. 76), "The true help that comes from God consists in his taking men and their actions seriously, incorporating them into his own operations." Paul said something similar when he wrote to the Christians in Philippi, "Work out your own salvation with fear and trembling; for God is at work in you, both to will and to work for [God's] good pleasure" (Phil. 2:12b–13).

Surely it is with this understanding of Jesus' call that we are to read such difficult biblical passages as Colossians 3:22, which bids slaves be obedient to their masters, as though they were obeying Christ himself. There is nothing in that passage that should be read as an approval of slavery. Rather, it is Paul's way of saying what we have been saying in this chapter: The workplace, whatever it may be, may become the scene of

God's being glorified through human activity. When Paul urges slaves to serve their masters well, slavery is not thereby sanctified. Rather it is shown to be what it is, a given part of the worldly order of things, which has no sanctity. It is *we* who are sanctified, made fit for divine service, by the call of Christ to faith and obedience, just as the fishermen were given roles in God's great drama of salvation.

In sum, to those who have heard the call of Christ, the workplace is a proving ground, a scene of high adventure. It is a place for making miraculous catches of fish, for turning water into wine, for walking on the sea, for turning the ordinary elements of life into that which serves God's purposes. The workplace is not a humdrum locale, where nothing ever happens; it is, potentially, the place where God's kingdom may become visible.

As Christ was present to the four by the Sea of Galilee, so is he present in the workplace you and I inhabit: kitchens, farms, offices, schools, factories, drilling grounds, laboratories, studios. As Jesus' call was to the fishermen, so it is to us—a call to high adventure.

3

The Call
to Perfection

You have heard that it was said, "An eye for an eye and a tooth for a tooth." But I say to you, Do not resist one who is evil. But if any one strikes you on the right cheek, turn to him the other also; and if any one would sue you and take your coat, let him have your cloak as well; and if any one forces you to go one mile, go with him two miles. Give to him who begs from you, and do not refuse him who would borrow from you.

You have heard that it was said, "You shall love your neighbor and hate your enemy." But I say to you, Love your enemies and pray for those who persecute you, so that you may be sons of your Father who is in heaven; for he makes his sun rise on the evil and on the good, and sends rain on the just and on the unjust. For if you love those who love you, what reward have you? Do not even the tax collectors do the same? And if you salute only your brethren, what more are you doing than others? Do not even the Gentiles do the same? You, therefore, must be perfect, as your heavenly Father is perfect.

—*Matthew 5:38–48*

In the movie *Witness* the central character is
John Book. He is a Philadelphia policeman who is
being hunted by his corrupt chief. John hides out
in an Amish community. One day, dressed in
Amish clothing, he goes with others to town,
where the Amishmen are taunted by young
toughs. Although he is told that striking back is
not the Amish way, he smashes one of the bullies
in the face, breaking his nose. Those watching the
film find it difficult not to feel righteous satisfaction at seeing the bully get "better than he gave."
However, the beating comes to the attention of the
local police and leads to John's chief finding where
he is hiding. The chief and his confederates invade
the Amish community with guns, and the matter
is not "settled" until there has been killing.

The incident reminds us of the imperfect nature
of justice in a none-too-perfect world. Certainly
there must be police, else the strong would prey on
the weak. Certainly there must be measured retribution—an eye for an eye, a tooth for a tooth—else
no eye or tooth would be safe. Yet the police may
be corrupted (John's chief was dealing in drugs)
and prey on the weak; and even "good cops" like
John Book exceed the limits of the law. A smashed
face is greater retribution than taunting deserves.

It is to disciples living in a world of imperfect
justice that Jesus issues his call to perfection:
"You, therefore, must be perfect, as your heavenly
Father is perfect." If you are insulted with a back-
hand to the face, you are not to seek retribution.
If you lose your shirt in a court case, give your
accuser your cloak as well. (Israelite law forbade
the judge to take away a poor man's cloak; it was
his only protection against the night's cold.) If a

soldier in an occupying army, exercising the right of conquest, forces you to carry his pack for a mile, carry it two.

Christians are to live in society in a manner that goes beyond nicely balancing rights and sanctions, injuries and restitutions. We are to seek a perfection that lies beyond the imperfections of human systems of law and order. Our goodness must exceed that of the John Books of this world.

A Counsel of Perfection?

What are we to make of Jesus' call to his disciples to practice such radical ethics in personal relations? Some have charged that this is a "counsel of perfection," which dooms anyone who tries to follow it to failure, guilt, and endless remorse. Such critics rightly argue that the chief bar to right behavior is self-hatred. Therefore, they contend, why add to that burden by laying on human beings a demand for goodness that is clearly beyond them? For a few who hanker after sainthood, the vision of such perfection may shine like a halo. For the rest of us it looks more like a crown of thorns.

That might be a fair indictment of Jesus' demands if we understood perfection as some kind of moral purity. Jesus does indeed acknowledge that he is asking for perfection; he says at the end of the passage, "You, therefore, must be perfect, as your heavenly Father is perfect." But the perfection he calls his disciples to achieve is not based on a moral ideal; rather, Jesus grounds his interpretation of the Law in God's own actions. As he says, "[God] makes his sun rise on the evil and on the

good, and sends rain on the just and on the unjust." God is not busy with vengeance on evildoers,
with keeping score, with evening things up.
Rather, God allows both the evil and the good to
have the benefit of daily sunshine and seasonal
rain.

And just as Jesus' understanding of God's perfection is not of some unapproachable holiness,
neither does Jesus demand of his disciples an impossible moral purity. The term "perfect" as Jesus
uses it means whole, intact, undivided. "It refers
to devotion to God, not to the flawlessness of a
rounded personality brought to the utmost pitch
of perfection. . . . Jesus calls God perfect not because God is aloof and totally unlike man, but
precisely the reverse: God is totally, undividedly
devoted to man; he is faithful to his covenant; he
is totally given to those he loves" (Schweizer, p.
135).

What Jesus calls the disciples to do is quite well
within the range of human behaviors that even
you and I can manage. He does not ask them—or
us—to walk on water or turn stones into bread. He
asks, rather, that when attacked we refrain from
retaliation; that we not settle our disputes in
courts of law; that we give to those who beg and
lend to those who would borrow, and that we pray
for our enemies. These are not easy things to do;
but they are not impossible. "To be perfect is not
the ideal of the monk; it is the obligation of every
Christian" (Meier, p. 55).

Take, for example, the injunction, "If any one
strikes you on the right cheek, turn to him the
other also." Gandhi built a massive political movement on the ability of ordinary persons to respond

to violence in a nonviolent manner; so did Martin Luther King, Jr. If civil rights activists could march from Selma to Montgomery under the threat of dogs and cattle prods and water hoses, cannot you and I take a slap in the face without slapping back?

Let us not fudge the matter: What we have in the fifth chapter of Matthew—as illustrated in the summons to turn the other cheek—is a call to perfection, a summons from Jesus to a kind of goodness, if you please, that reflects the very goodness of God. Made in God's image, we are to behave in a way that gives God credit for God's behavior! "God thus resembles a mold, for man's clay to conform to" (Schweizer, p. 135). Jesus calls for human behavior grounded in the actions of God. "We love, because [God] first loved us" is the way the writer of the First Epistle of John put it (1 John 4:19).

Let us be clear: Jesus' plea that we not resist evildoers is not the statement of a universal ideal or a moral principle. Rather it is what in this book we have termed a call. Like the summons to the fishermen to leave their normal occupation, the call to nonresistance is a summons to behave in a way that is not normal for human beings. For the natural instinct of us all is to strike back, to exact revenge, to get even, to keep score.

When I was a seminary student, I spent a summer as counselor at a boys' camp. We tried to give to kids who spent much of their lives on the sidewalks of New York a notion of what the new life in Christ was about, and that meant a brief devotional period after lights out. One night I gave to the fourteen-year-olds in my cabin a brief exposi-

tion of the Sermon on the Mount, including the
injunction to "turn the other cheek." No sooner
had I finished speaking when a potato came flying
in the door and struck Rimmler on the side of the
head. He leaped from his bunk and fired the potato
back at the tent across the way. Thus began the
Great Potato War, which raged unchecked for the
better part of an hour. The natural man—or boy—
responds to a blow on the cheek by seeking to
return that blow, with interest!

God displays very unhuman characteristics in
allowing rain and sun to fall on the just and the
unjust. What's more, God displays divine mercy in
actively reaching out to pardon evil and injustice!
In the eleventh chapter of Hosea, the prophet
represents God as repenting of punishment that
had been planned for Israel. God says:

> I will not execute my fierce anger,
>   I will not again destroy Ephraim;
> for I am God and not man,
>   the Holy One in your midst,
>   and I will not come to destroy.
>   —Hosea 11:9

The heart of God is not so much reflected in
sunshine and rain as it is in the cross, where God
literally turned the other cheek to the enemies of
goodness and justice. Jesus, the obedient son, fulfilled the words of the prophet:

> I gave my back to the smiters,
>   and my cheeks to those who pulled out the beard.
>   —Isaiah 50:6

If you and I want to be called sons and daughters of God, we are to act in the same way.

Our Call

Our call, then, as believers in Jesus Christ and members of his church, is to act toward others as God has acted toward us: to turn the other cheek, to offer no active resistance to evil actions. We are not to try to even the score when we are wronged; rather, we are to refuse to keep going the endless cycle of crime, revenge, more crime, more revenge. Moreover, we are to actively pray for our enemies—those who rob us, strike us, revile us, and wish us ill.

If I am verbally assaulted in a meeting, I am not to repay in kind. If someone knocks me aside in crowding into the subway car, I am not to push back. If there is a neighbor whose dislike for me is exhibited in small annoyances, I am to pretend that nothing is amiss. Moreover, I am to pray for my enemies. Those people whom I love to hate, upon whom in my fantasies I exact such sweet revenge, I am to ask God to bless!

It is important, in discussing this highly controversial passage from the Sermon on the Mount, that we pause here to say clearly what this call of Jesus is *not* about: It is *not* a promise that if we treat others in a nonviolent way they will treat us in a similar fashion. The call is grounded not in the nature or propensity of human beings but in the behavior of God. Nor is it a command to create, through law or practice, a nonviolent society. It is not even a general rule about nonresistance to all evil. "The doctrine of absolute non-resistance to evil is not enunciated here: the issue is one of individual conduct in specific circumstances" (Hill, p. 127). It is a call to Christians, who live in a violent and revenge-filled world, to shun retaliation and revenge and to show appreciation for God's patience and mercy by showing patience and mercy.

It is also useful to put the call to nonresistance to evil in historical context. What Jesus did was to move a long step beyond the ancient *lex talionis,* the law of revenge, which sought to limit retaliation to proportionate degrees: *only* "an eye for an eye and a tooth for a tooth." Most contemporary systems of justice are built upon a similar notion: The punishment for a violent crime should be proportional to the offense. If a man robs me, he is to spend time in jail; he is not to be executed. If a man steps on my toe, I am entitled to an apology; not to having his foot cut off!

Jesus went beyond this ancient and honorable notion that vengeance is to be proportional to the offense. His call to his disciples was to give up the notion of the proportional response, to forswear revenge, to break the old cycle of wrong-punishment-wrong-punishment. And that was grounded on the action and character of God, not on any optimistic notion of human nature. If God lets the needed rains fall on evil and good, just and unjust, we are to behave in like manner.

Of course, one must believe that indeed God "sends rain on the just and on the unjust" alike! One could decide that God has not been playing fair with his rain and take matters into one's own hands. My wife and I were on an archaeological dig in the Southwest in which the indisputable evidence was that members of one village had killed and burned the inhabitants of a neighboring village—and had then built their own homes upon the burned bones and charred roofs of their neighbors. The only explanation that the archaeologist could give was this: The rains had fallen unevenly upon the fields of these peoples. Those upon whose fields the rains had not fallen had decided that their more favored neighbors were practicing witchcraft; why else would some fields be blessed with rain while adjacent fields went dry?

Whenever I am angry at someone, I hope I remember those villages and what happened. It is very easy, when one is wronged, to suppose that the fault is no accident, that the person who was the agent of the hurt is himself or herself "wrong"—and to let ourselves become instruments of God's justice instead of imitators of God's mercy. How quick we are to undertake to redress what God or nature has done amiss! If we are unhappy or unlucky or miserable, someone must be to blame. Almost any hurt or slight will be an excuse for violent retaliation, out of all proportion to the hurt or slight. And like the villagers on our mountain site in New Mexico, we take out after the others with vengeance. Since we are "good" and the others are "evil," nothing we can do is to be faulted. To those heavens from which rain has fallen unevenly, we cry for vengeance—and to those heavens we look for vindication for our actions.

Against this excess, to which all humans are prone, Jesus protested. Better to suffer a blow, a deprivation, an insult than to make oneself the agent of God's wrath and justice.

In *Lords of the Plain,* a novel about cavalry actions in Texas, Max Crawford puts these words into the mouth of the defense attorney for Comanche braves on trial for the massacre of a wagon train:

> "I will now speak to you of reason and mercy, of forgiveness and understanding. I will speak to you against violence and hatred, against blind passion and brute strength. I will speak to you of vengeance and its folly. I will speak to you of wrongs begetting wrongs till there be no end to wrongs. I will speak to you of making ourselves good men, strong and gentle, who will put an end to our war and vengeance and stupid, stupid bloodshed. I will speak to you of the way we are now and of the way that we may yet be."

This plea follows a long description of the wrongs and hurts suffered by the Scots-Irish forebears of the members of the jury, and of the hurts these forebears had laid on others in return.

History is rich in examples of the futility of trying to "even the score." The current state of affairs in the Middle East is another case in point: Both Israeli and Arab have decided that the only justice to be had is "An eye for an eye and a tooth for a tooth." But somehow the violence returned upon the doer of violence is never quite proportional; someone innocent always gets caught in the crossfire. And that innocent one is turned into an agent of vengeance.

Not that Jesus promised that if we turned the

other cheek we would create a society of nonviolence! I once stepped between two army buddies who were pounding on each other; all I got for my pains were a couple of blows to the head. Rather, Jesus seems to have seen that "an eye for an eye" does not deliver the justice it seems to promise; like the command of Moses to allow divorce, it was given men "because of their hardness of heart." But it was not grounded in the action of God, and so had to be superseded.

One might well interject that most of us—unless we go about meddling in the quarrels of others—are not in much danger of being slapped in the face. So should we not seek to extract from this passage in Matthew some general rules for conduct, some program of nonviolence, an ethics of pacifism perhaps?

No. Let us take the commands of Jesus as concrete, specific calls to obedience. If in the course of an ordinary day we are not struck in the face or accosted by beggars or taken to court or hit up for a loan, there are plenty of other demands on our time for faithful living! However, there is one item in the list of commands that most of us can do every day of our lives: Pray for our enemies.

When he leads persons in a study of our passage from the Sermon on the Mount, master teacher Walter Wink asks them to do the following: Bring into consciousness an enemy; conduct an imaginary dialogue with that person, in which you accuse him or her of the evil he or she seems to intend, imagining what he or she might say in response; then pray for the well-being of that person. In such a spiritual exercise, one finds oneself both nearer to God and farther from perfection

than one would like! However, one finds that it is
possible to pray for one's enemies. And in the act
of praying, the enemy becomes more like oneself,
less a threat, less a terror.

I have an alcoholic friend who was sent off for
a time to a sanitarium to dry out. When he was
gone, his workmates tried to get him fired; only
the determined action of his wife saved his job.
When he returned, he brought a violent hatred
of those who had wished him harm. Although he
started to pray for them, for the first month all
he could do was to curse them before God. But
eventually he found that he could pray for their
well-being, and his rage and wrath became man-
ageable.

In this chapter, I have dealt chiefly with one of
Jesus' illustrations of what it means to "be perfect, as your heavenly Father is perfect." We are
to "turn the other cheek" and to pray for those
who persecute us. The same case could be made for
the commands to give more than is demanded in
a court settlement, to go the second mile, to give
to beggars, to give to borrowers. These, too, are
calls to perfection. The call is not confined to the
areas of law and order but to all of social relationships. "Jesus demolishes all the fences into which
men would confine love of neighbor" (Schweizer,
p. 133).

Jesus' call to perfection is a summons to act as
God acts. In matters of justice and retribution, we
are to follow the example of One who is not our
implacable judge but who pronounces us—the
guilty ones—as innocent. As our heavenly Father
is perfect, so are we to be perfect. It is the least we
can do for God.

4

The Call to Secret Service

Beware of practicing your piety before men in order to be seen by them; for then you will have no reward from your Father who is in heaven.

Thus, when you give alms, sound no trumpet before you, as the hypocrites do in the synagogues and in the streets, that they may be praised by men. Truly, I say to you, they have received their reward. But when you give alms, do not let your left hand know what your right hand is doing, so that your alms may be in secret; and your Father who sees in secret will reward you.

And when you pray, you must not be like the hypocrites; for they love to stand and pray in the synagogues and at the street corners, that they may be seen by men. Truly, I say to you, they have received their reward. But when you pray, go into your room and shut the door and pray to your Father who is in secret; and your Father who sees in secret will reward you.

And in praying do not heap up empty phrases as the Gentiles do; for they think that they will be heard for their many words. Do not be like them, for your Father knows what you need before you ask him. Pray then like this:

Our Father who art in heaven,
Hallowed be thy name.
Thy kingdom come,
Thy will be done,
   On earth as it is in heaven.
Give us this day our daily bread;
And forgive us our debts,
   As we also have forgiven our debtors;
And lead us not into temptation,
But deliver us from evil.

For if you forgive men their trespasses, your heavenly Father also will forgive you; but if you do not forgive men their trespasses, neither will your Father forgive your trespasses.

And when you fast, do not look dismal, like the hypocrites, for they disfigure their faces that their fasting may be seen by men. Truly, I say to you, they have received their reward. But when you fast, anoint your head and wash your face, that your fasting may not be seen by men but by your Father who is in secret; and your Father who sees in secret will reward you.

—Matthew 6:1–18

An oxymoron is a descriptive phrase containing a logical contradiction: a deafening silence, a cold fire, or, my daughter's favorite, military intelligence. To say that Christ calls us to a private piety is to venture an oxymoron. For what is piety if not a public display? A secret service of God seems a contradiction in terms. To pray only in the privacy of one's room; to be so secretive in giving to charity that the left hand does not know the right hand is writing a check; to tell no one, not even one's spouse, that one is fasting—what kind of piety is that?

And yet that seems the clear call that Jesus issued to his disciples and, through them, to us. That which the world calls piety we are to practice in secret. There is to be absolutely no public show of praying, almsgiving, or fasting. Such things are to be treated as private matters—as private as one's sexual conduct. There is a secret service that we may render to God, which no other need know about. Like CIA operatives in a foreign country, whose cover masks a hidden identity and a hidden task, so are we to conceal our religious practices from the world.

Among the Jews of Jesus' time, there were religious duties that one could perform above and beyond the keeping of the law; their justification was that they were pleasing to God. These were prayer, almsgiving, and fasting. These, said Jesus, were to be done as private matters; piety—the practice of purely religious duties—was to be a secret service to God.

That piety should be a private matter is a radical not to say revolutionary idea. It goes totally against the cultural grain. For traditional piety is something performed for others to see. In Roman culture, *pietas* referred to the public veneration of the gods. Without such a display from prominent citizens, what would happen to the traditional values that were associated with the gods? *Pietas* was the cultural glue, holding all things in place. How could there be law and order without it?

In our own generation we are witness to the same practice: Persons who hold public office are careful in their speeches to make occasional refer-

ence to the Deity and to be photographed going to
their church or synagogue. Such utterances and
practices are clearly nonsectarian. Their purpose
is not to enunciate a doctrine or air a belief or bear
a testimony; their purpose is to exhibit piety. We
do not want our public officials to preach at us, but
we do want to be assured that they are godly men
and women and that ours is a society that ac-
knowledges the rule of God.

From what Jesus says in Matthew 6:1–18 about
his own society, we can assume that public displays of piety were quite common. People made a
great show of praying, almsgiving, and fasting.
Then, as now, it was taken for granted that one
would make a show of performing one's religious
duties. Men would stand in the street and offer
prayers. In the synagogues announcements were
made of gifts to the poor; very large gifts were
signaled by the blast of a trumpet. And those who
fasted cultivated a lean and famished look, that
others would know the extent of their self-depriva-
tion.

This insistence on winning public recognition
for one's piety Jesus found offensive; he called it
hypocrisy. He said that those who made a public
show of religious duties received a very limited
reward: They received the approval of others. But
the reward they hoped for—to be found pleasing
to God—would be denied them. Jesus did not condemn the practices of prayer, almsgiving, or fasting. But he disapproved of their practice as a
public show. He pointed out that, like snapshots
on a camera film accidentally exposed to light,
they were ruined by disclosure.

The Father in Secret

Jesus' call to a secret service of God was based upon his relationship to the Father who sees in secret. Three times he promised that the person whose piety was practiced in private would be rewarded by "your Father who sees in secret." Like the author of Psalm 139, Jesus knew the One who sees in secret (v. 2):

> Thou knowest when I sit down and when I rise up;
> Thou discernest my thoughts from afar.

This One who knows our innermost thoughts deserves a secret service.

God is not, strictly speaking, hidden from us; in Christ, God has disclosed the divine heart and intention. And yet there is also a sense in which God both knows and is known in secret. There is a private, reciprocal knowledge of God. It is to this One who knows our secret thoughts that we direct our piety.

In fact, we may infer from what Jesus says that God is secretly pleased with prayer, almsgiving, and fasting when it is done not for any approval of our fellow human beings—or even with their knowledge—but only for the eyes and ears of God. Jesus would have applauded the woman in the legend who went about with a bucket of hot coals in one hand and a bucket of water in the other. When asked what she intended, she said, "I want to burn up heaven and put out the fires of hell so that persons will love God for God's goodness alone, with no fear of punishment or hope of reward!"

But is it possible to love God in a private way? Some may object that to approve of a secret service is to cut the vital nerve between love of God and love of neighbor. Is not the genius of both Judaism and Christianity a holy triangle, in which love of God and love of neighbor are separate but never separated activities? Did not Jesus say that we are lights in this world? Are we not to act so that others "may see [our] good works and give glory to [our] Father who is in heaven" (Matt. 5:16)? And what of the accusation that not only private but also *individual* piety—prayer, almsgiving, fasting—is a retreat from the real world? Isn't advocacy of a secret service an invitation to private religion, an avoidance of our duties to the poor and oppressed?

To those objections one needs to respond gently but firmly that such service is pleasing to the Father in heaven. The Greek word that is translated as "piety" in Matthew 6:1 is the same word that is translated as "righteousness" in 5:20. And behind that Greek word lies the Hebrew word for justice. We owe to God both a public service and a private one; one cannot slip a knife between civic virtues and the life of devotion and say that one is pleasing to God and the other is not. It may be difficult for us modern folk to see any casual connection between prayer and politics, but that is our problem! As the author of Matthew reports in this passage, God knows and sees, and that is all that matters. If one would rightly serve the unseen God, one performs acts of piety in ways that avoid being seen. For that is the only way to avoid the trap of hypocrisy. Religion has a built-in hazard: Believers are tempted to be good for the show of it. (The Greek word *hypokritēs* means "actor.") The only way to avoid the trap of hypocrisy is to shun all public spectacles of piety. God sees in secret and rewards in secret.

This reading of Matthew 6:1–18 does not find universal agreement. Eduard Schweizer says (p. 142) that "the man who really places his confidence in God renounces all righteousness that can be judged by men, even by the agent himself; he thus escapes the notion of any accomplishment that would earn reward in the eyes of God."

But to accept that notion one has to discard all that Matthew says in 6:1–18 about rewards. Besides, as Schweizer himself points out, in Romans 2:28–29 Paul also draws a distinction between what is done for show and what is done for God. John Meier seems closer to the intent of the Gospel author when he writes (p. 57), "The stress on the heavenly Father puts the reward idea—which is indeed part of Jesus' moral exhortation—into the context of a gift a Father gives his son, and not a strict wage an employer is bound to give his employee."

Our Call to Prayer

Probably the most difficult aspect of this secret service is the call to private prayer. Jesus bid us, when we pray, to go into our room and shut out the rest of the world. We are not to pray to a public God, who is present in the marketplace and meetinghouse. The Father sees in secret; we are to pray to God in secret.

Those, then, who set themselves up as experts in prayer, who hold workshops, make a public dis-

play of a private matter. They are like radio talk-
show hosts who chatter with callers about their
sex lives. Normal human beings, overhearing such
stuff on the public airwaves, must feel that they
have blundered into someone else's bedroom una-
wares.

A person's prayers are a private matter between
that person and God. We ought never be stopped
on the street and asked about our prayer life! If
you have trouble praying, go to your pastor and
ask for help. But the pastor ought to be as discreet
in giving advice about prayer as in advising about
making love. Your pastor—no less than you—is
tempted by the exhibitionism against which Jesus
warned.

Besides, as Jesus pointed out, prayer is no big
deal. God knows what we need before we ask, even
as parents know the wants of their children. We
do not need to heap up long and tiresome phrases
to get God's attention or to move God to action.
Prayer is simple and straightforward. Jesus gave
us a model for prayer that is also a model of brev-
ity. It consists of six terse petitions: that God's
name be hallowed, God's kingdom come, God's
will be done, and that we receive bread, forgiveness, and help in the face of evil. Period. End of
teaching about prayer. All we need to know.

To his model, Jesus attached a promise: "If you
forgive men their trespasses, your heavenly Father also will forgive you." It is a reminder that
there is no magic in the words Jesus taught us;
prayer requires integrity. If we ask for forgiveness, we ourselves are to be forgiving. The rationale for that is spelled out later in the Gospel in

the Parable of the Unforgiving Servant. Jesus tells the story of a servant who forfeited his king's forgiveness of a great debt because he could not forgive a fellow servant a paltry debt. And one supposes likewise that if a woman prays for daily bread, she ought to be ready to share bread with the neighbor who has none. And if a man prays to be delivered from evil, he ought to avoid leading others astray.

The Call to Almsgiving

What might it mean to give alms to the poor in such a way that one's left hand did not know what one's right hand was doing? For such is Jesus' admonition about personal charity; it is to be private, in the most strict sense. "Alms are given for the sake of the poor, not for personal satisfaction" (Hill, p. 133). Jesus gives us a negative description: One is not to insist on public recognition for one's benevolence. There is a social recognition for benefaction that is the equivalent of having one's name and donation read aloud in the synagogue, to the accompaniment of trumpets. Published lists of donors, the announcement of pledges to the church building fund campaign, the insistence on a tax write-off for a donation—all these would seem to belong to the kind of public display that Jesus decried.

Should Christians then not report on their IRS forms the amounts they have given to charity? It would seem to violate the spirit of Jesus' call; it is spiritual double-dipping. One seeks to please a generous God and act in God's likeness, respond-

ing to the needs of others with an open hand. And
yet, since one can also get credit with the IRS, why
not? Why not indeed?

What is at stake is the enormous temptation to
demand credit—in the form of the approval of others—for faithful behavior. We were brought up to
please our earthly fathers; they rewarded us when
we did well; we learned how wonderful it is to get
approval for good behavior. And the temptation
lies close at hand to behave in the same way in
prayer, fasting, and almsgiving; we like the feeling of being approved by others. But how should
we need such credit when our debts have already
been paid? If God has forgiven our sins, is not
gratitude for such grace to displace in our hearts
the demand for credit?

A first reading of Matthew 6:1–18 does indeed
give the impression that there is a heavenly book-
keeping system, in which good deeds are credited
in the heavenly account. Jesus speaks of faithful
behavior being rewarded by the Father who sees
in secret. But of course God does not keep books!
If there is one lesson that scripture teaches, it is
that God does not keep books, with pluses and
minuses beside each name. God who is our Judge
is at once and the same time our Redeemer. All
accounts have been marked *Paid.* That is our only
hope. None of us has the slightest chance of getting off for good behavior. So whatever Jesus
means by rewards from the heavenly Father, it
cannot be any kind of credit in God's accounting
system. Rather it must mean that such actions are
pleasing to God, a suitable thanksgiving to God for
grace and mercy given us. Since we cannot give
God anything tangible, we give alms to the poor

and needy. That God is touched and pleased by such kindness is our one and only reward!

The Call to Fasting

Fasting has nearly ceased to be practiced among us as a religious duty; it has been replaced by other forms of self-denial. One of the most common of those among us is dieting, which is largely cosmetic and therapeutic. What is there to say about it? Perhaps only this: How much happier we should all be if persons who diet would just shut up about it! Let dieting be as private a matter as prayer and almsgiving. The couplet that used to be quoted to those who quit smoking could well be modified and recited for dieters:

> Giving up eating too much isn't enough,
> It's giving up bragging about it that's tough.

In sum, Jesus calls us to a personal piety that is wholly private. We are to go about prayer and almsgiving and self-denial as though we were enlisted in the divine Secret Service. No one seeing us is to know that we are about such things. In fact, Eduard Schweizer suggests (p. 146), to anoint your head and wash your face when you fast is "to act as if going to a feast." In other words, to go about it in disguise. Søren Kierkegaard, the Danish theologian, has a passage in which he describes the faithful Christian: "Good heavens," says Kierkegaard, "he looks like a tax collector." To outward appearance, the Christian is no different from the most ordinary and mundane of persons.

It is not easy to let one's piety be hidden! If one

has a lovely voice and sings in a church choir, the
temptation is almost irresistible to let one's voice
sound out above the others. "Listen to me. Is not
my voice beautiful? Am I not fortunate to have
such a musical instrument?" What's more, it is so
satisfying to let one's golden tones ring out above
the ordinary noises made by fellow singers! To
know that others are hearing the same lovely
voice that rings in one's own ears; what could be
sweeter? But is God glorified by such a display?
No, said Jesus, one does not need public validation. If a tree falls in the forest and no one hears
it, is there truly a sound? If one transposes that to
the life of faithfulness, the answer is a solid yes.
The hearing or seeing by others is not what makes
our acts faithful. It is the faithfulness of God that
is our validation. To serve such a One is our calling.

There will be some who will want to be rid of
piety altogether, be it private or public. When
Karl Marx spoke scornfully of religion as the opi-
ate of the people, no doubt he had in mind the
practices of prayer, almsgiving, and fasting; these,
he said, diverted attention from matters of social
justice and gave people a good conscience when
their conscience ought to be troubled.

But we ought never be ashamed of the push or
pull of piety. It should be enough for us that God
is pleased with our prayers, our alms, our self-
denial. To try to live wholly without reference to
the Father who sees in secret is neither desirable
nor possible. We must have our dreams, our
myths, our prayers, our worship, our angels, our
sacred book. A human being who has no referent
outside of herself or himself is an animal, no more.

Modern films and fiction are replete with examples of persons who try to live as though there were no unseen God, and such persons have the look and smell of monsters. Our calling is not to live wholly in this world, and for this world, but to live in this world as children of the Father who sees and is known in secret—but not to let that relationship become a matter of exhibitionism and the occasion for public approval. That is a high calling indeed!

The clinching argument for a secret service of God is Jesus' Parable of the Pharisee and the Publican, Luke 18:9–14. Jesus tells of two men who go up to the temple for prayer. One man practices the three religious virtues that have been discussed in this chapter. Not only do we see him at prayer, but he says of himself, "I fast twice a week, I give tithes of all that I get." He is a Pharisee, a member of a religious group that strove for exemplary piety. The other man is a tax collector, whose public image is that of a corrupt official. We feel some sympathy for the Pharisee when he congratulates himself that he is not like other men—extortioners, unjust, adulterers, tax collectors. When the tax collector beats his breast and moans, "God, be merciful to me a sinner!" we are not surprised. We can only hope that God will, in the divine mercy, soften the man's punishment.

And yet Jesus said of the tax collector, "This man went down to his house justified rather than the other." Why? For the very reason that the term "Pharisee" has become interchangeable with the term "hypocrite." The effort to lead a life of public piety had made the first man self-congratulatory, self-justifying, judgmental of others.

He had fallen into the trap that we have described at some length in this exposition of Matthew 6:1–18. Perhaps the word "quicksand" would be more accurate than "trap." For the nature of piety is such that the more one struggles to live an exemplary life, the deeper one sinks into hypocrisy.

Those who are called to follow Jesus will never aspire, in their private lives, to a piety that goes deeper than the daily confession, "God, have mercy on me a sinner." They will be content to have others look and say, "Are these Christians? Good heavens, they look like tax collectors!"

5

The Call
to Mirror a Ministry

*And Jesus went about all the cities and villages,
teaching in their synagogues and preaching the
gospel of the kingdom, and healing every disease
and every infirmity. When he saw the crowds, he
had compassion for them, because they were
harassed and helpless, like sheep without a shep-
herd. Then he said to his disciples, "The harvest is
plentiful, but the laborers are few; pray therefore
the Lord of the harvest to send out laborers into his
harvest."*

*And he called to him his twelve disciples and
gave them authority over unclean spirits, to cast
them out, and to heal every disease and every infirmity. The names of the twelve apostles are these:
first, Simon, who is called Peter, and Andrew his
brother; James the son of Zebedee, and John his
brother; Philip and Bartholomew; Thomas and
Matthew the tax collector; James the son of Al-
phaeus, and Thaddaeus; Simon the Cananaean,
and Judas Iscariot, who betrayed him.*

*These twelve Jesus sent out, charging them, "Go
nowhere among the Gentiles, and enter no town of
the Samaritans, but go rather to the lost sheep of
the house of Israel. And preach as you go, saying,*

*'The kingdom of heaven is at hand.' Heal the sick,
raise the dead, cleanse lepers, cast out demons."*
— *Matthew 9:35–10:8a*

Are you and I called to go hand to hand with
death, disease, and demons? Does God want us to
revivify corpses, restore fingers and toes to those
afflicted with leprosy, and exorcise evil spirits? If
we read Matthew 9:35–10:8a in the straightforward way we have read other narratives, such
would be the clear implications.

As Matthew tells his story, Jesus had been
doing his characteristic works of preaching and
healing. There was far more work than he could
do alone. So he called twelve intimate friends and
empowered them to preach and heal. It seems
clear enough that in Matthew's Gospel the Twelve
are meant to represent the church. So it follows
that you and I—members of the church—are likewise called and commissioned to perform marvelous works.

You will get little argument among Christians
that we are called to teach and preach in Jesus'
name. Then why should we not expect to follow his
example in doing marvelous works of healing? For
Jesus had a dual ministry: He announced the present realm of God; and, as signs and seals of the
veracity of that announcement, he performed extraordinary labors of healing and exorcism. Or, if
you prefer, he did works of mercy and explained
their meaning by the announcement, "The kingdom of heaven is at hand." In a dramatic demonstration that the kingdom of heaven meant the
defeat of the powers of evil and death, Jesus raised
the dead, cleansed lepers, and cast out evil spirits.

And as is clearly stated in the passage from Matthew that is under consideration, Jesus gave to his disciples the authority to do that same dual work. It was this empowerment that turned disciples into apostles. Learners became like their Teacher, servants like their Master. Even after Jesus ascended into heaven, the apostles continued to both preach and do wonderful signs in his name. The Acts of the Apostles records a number of these, such as the healing of the lame man in the temple by John and Peter, described in the third chapter of Acts.

What of Us?

What of us twentieth-century Christians? Are we called to do the same? Are we to both preach and do miracles? Or are we to remain forever as disciples, willing to watch what Jesus did, and even tell others about it, but never ourselves to take up his ministry? Are we not members of a church that calls itself apostolic and claims spiritual descent from the Twelve? And therefore are we not, in the twentieth century, called to complete what Jesus started in the first century? If our Sovereign went hand to hand with death, disease, and demons, on what grounds do we ask deferment?

Here, at midpoint in our consideration of Christ's call, a fearful question hangs quivering in the air, a question that offends the sensibilities of cultured, reasonable people: *Are we Christians called by Christ to hand-to-hand combat with the powers of death, disease, and demonology?*

We cannot offer an unequivocal yes or no to that

question—not without being found to be liars. For
if we say flatly yes, it must be with the full knowledge that there are no contemporary referents for
"raise the dead" and "cast out demons." If we say
that we are called to such marvelous works, we
are affirming an imperative that is impossible for
us to obey. We cannot raise corpses from coffins,
nor do we believe in the existence of demons—not
the kind that invade human bodies. So if we say
yes indeed, we are called to such works, it has got
to be with our fingers crossed or our tongues in our
cheeks.

But neither dare we offer a flat no, for then we
are being false to God's word. The New Testament
affirms that, in Christ, God won a victory for us
over the powers of death, disease, and evil. If
Christ is not somehow Sovereign of these awful
powers, he is not Sovereign at all. Having confessed Jesus Christ as Sovereign, we do not want
so openly to deny him. Besides, in this study of
Matthew we have taken other calling narratives
as imperative for us. How should we now suddenly
decide to duck a call because it seems impossible
to obey? Somehow we must interpret Matthew
9:35–10:8a so as to preserve it as a calling narrative—but in a way that makes it possible for us to
obey it.

To repeat, there is no way the call to the Twelve
can be heard by us exactly like other calls. For we
cannot obey commands to "raise the dead" and
"cast out demons." Not that these are meaning-
less commands. On three separate occasions Jesus
is described in the Gospels as bringing back to life
persons who had died: the son of the widow of
Nain, the daughter of Jairus, and Lazarus. In the

book of Acts, Peter raises Dorcas from the state of death. Also in the Gospels are a number of accounts of the exorcism of evil spirits—demons, if you will.

Without denying that such things happened as the Bible describes them, still we cannot understand what it would mean today for us to "raise the dead" or "cast out demons." Such performances are not part of our worldview. Perceptions limit actions. We cannot do what we cannot imagine ourselves doing. Korean shamans may very well drive out evil spirits. But you and I do not believe in evil spirits. Who among us can imagine himself or herself acting the part of the shaman?

We can imagine others raising the dead. There is a pastor of a charismatic congregation in Seoul, Korea, who is purported to have revived his son after the child was pronounced dead. We listen to such accounts with skepticism, but we are not forced to deny them outright. Since we have heard the biblical stories of Jesus and the apostles raising the dead, we can imagine others doing so. *But you and I cannot seriously imagine ourselves doing likewise.*

Therefore we cannot offer a flat yes to the question: Are we called to go hand to hand with death, disease, and demons? But neither can we offer an unequivocal no—at least not until we have explored every possible avenue of explanation. For by what right do we pick and choose among calls, heeding some and ignoring others? Does it not belong to the very nature of a divine call that it comes from beyond our limited world and demands that we go beyond the bounds of the ordinary?

So let us then patiently and carefully explore what imperative there might be for us in Jesus' call to the Twelve to heal the sick, raise the dead, cleanse lepers, and cast out demons.

Avenues for Exploration

What we need is a metaphor—a figure of speech—that will mediate between the literal meaning of Jesus' call and our contemporary understanding of the world. We find such a metaphor supplied by John P. Meier. All four of our commentators agree that the call to the Twelve was to continue Jesus' ministry in the world. But Meier supplies a liberating metaphor when he writes (p. 107), "The mission of the disciples mirrors that of Jesus in word and work." The word "mirrors" supplies the metaphor. Our words and works are to mirror the words and works of Jesus. We are not called to imitate Jesus as a child seeks to imitate a parent, nor are we called to obey him in the manner of soldiers obeying a direct order. Rather, our actions are to mirror those of Jesus.

The metaphor is suggestive: To mirror the activity of another is to *respond* to that person's words and actions. Jesus acts and speaks; we act and speak in appropriate response. To mirror the activity of another is also to *amplify* it. Before the days of radio and telegraph, messages could be flashed by mirror from watchtower to watchtower, covering great distances. Our actions serve to enlarge the ministry of Jesus across time and space. To mirror is also to *reflect.* A mirror does not create images, it only passes them along; a mirror can only function on borrowed light; it has no power of its own to illumine. Jesus takes the initiative; we act and speak in ways that are appropriate to his actions and words.

Once we are freed by the metaphor from a literal interpretation of Jesus' call to ministry, a number of possibilities—at least five—open to us.

First of all, we may say that in our personal lives we are called upon to resist the powers of death, disease, and evil. We know from our own experience and from the arts and literature how common it is for humans to be ruled by these powers. In *The Denial of Death,* Ernest Becker demonstrates how much of our behavior can be described as an unconscious effort to cope with the certain knowledge that we must die. How many persons do you know whose whole lives are circumscribed by illness? To throw oneself into a personal struggle against the powers of death and disease in one's own life is a way of responding to Jesus' call to struggle against death, disease, and demons. Our personal lives—as we struggle for health and sanity and goodness—mirror Jesus' struggle against disease and death.

A second and more sophisticated interpretation is this: We are called to attack boldly and forthrightly the structural powers of death, disease, and evil. The fear of nuclear annihilation, under which many live, can be attacked by efforts to rid the world of nuclear weapons. Disease becomes endemic and epidemic in the form of AIDS; one can join all-out efforts to rid the world of AIDS. Racism is an obsession as pernicious and devilish as any possession by evil spirits of first-century people; we can do everything within our powers to oppose racism.

Third, we can liken the marvelous works to which Jesus called the Twelve to the heroic, super-human efforts made by individual Christians to combat the powers of death, disease, and evil. One thinks of Mother Teresa fighting on the side of the dying in Calcutta, or William Wilberforce in nine-teenth-century England taking on the slave trade, or Martin Luther King, Jr., attacking racism in America. They serve as mirrors of the Master.

There is also a fourth possibility—that the ex-traordinary works to which Jesus calls his church are of the order of working for the positive values of which death, disease, and demon possession rep-resent the negatives. One could say that Jesus calls his followers to work for life fulfillment, health, and education for all God's children. There are various ways in which the church has entered the lists on the side of humanity and fought for better health systems, schools, mental health pro-grams, and the like.

The Fifth Possibility

None of those possibilities rules out or cancels out the others. Any or all of them may operate simultaneously. But there is a fifth possibility, which may obtain in, with, and under any or all the others. And that is the possibility that the marvelous works to which Jesus calls us are the celebration of the sacraments of Baptism and the Lord's Supper.

There are two strong hints in Matthew 9:35–10:8a that this indeed may be the case. There is the fact that the extraordinary labors that Jesus performed—and authorized his disciples to perform—were signs that accompanied the preaching of God's kingdom. The healing miracles were not so much proofs as they were visible demonstrations. If one wanted a demonstration of what it meant that "the kingdom of heaven is at hand," one saw the dead being raised, lepers cleansed, evil spirits driven out, and persons healed of various diseases. In the activity of Jesus, God could be seen putting human affairs to rights, entering the lists on behalf of humans against their ancient enemies.

When John the Baptist sent to ask Jesus if he were indeed the One who was to come, Jesus sent back this answer: "Go and tell John what you hear and see: the blind receive their sight and the lame walk, lepers are cleansed and the deaf hear, and the dead are raised up, and the poor have good news preached to them" (Matt. 11:4–5). In Jesus' ministry there was both a spoken word and an acted witness, with neither word nor deed standing alone or serving merely to illustrate or prove the other.

The entire Gospel of John is one in which word and deed (sign) are so bound together they cannot be separated. The Gospel begins with the announcement that in the beginning was the Word, and the Word came to dwell with humankind. And then the Gospel proceeds to describe the presence among us of that Word by the narration of a series of signs: the turning of water to wine at the wedding in Cana, the feeding of the five thousand, the healing of the man born blind, the raising of Lazarus.

In our interpretation of Matthew 9:35–10:8a we are making great concessions to modern percep-

tions; we are trying to accommodate Gospel imper-
atives to what we moderns can and cannot imagine ourselves doing. But that should not allow us
to impose twentieth-century ways of thinking
upon first-century minds. We tend to drive a
wedge between word and deed. Words, we say, are
mental abstractions, while deeds are concrete
events. Words are not deeds; deeds are not words.
We want to pry the two apart and keep them
apart. But one cannot understand the New Testament if one insists on doing that. Word and deed
belong somehow together; Jesus' teachings reveal
the meaning of his actions; his actions explain the
import of his teachings. And when one asks, What
signs (acted words) did Jesus leave to his church to
stand alongside the preaching and teaching? the
answer that comes to mind is the sacraments of
Baptism and the Lord's Supper!

Matthew 9:35–10:8a offers us another clue that
the sacraments may be marvelous works that
Jesus calls his church to do. There is indication
that the works of raising the dead and casting out
demons belong exclusively to the time of Jesus'
presence in the flesh. When he sent out the Twelve
to do marvelous things, he charged them strictly
to do such things only for the eyes and ears of "the
house of Israel." They were forbidden to do them
for Gentiles, even for Samaritans. These signs, it
would seem, had a particularly revelatory purpose: They were, in the minds of witnessing Jews,
to link Jesus with the Old Testament revelation.
They were not, in other words, part of the worldwide mission of the church; other signs were to be
given to serve that purpose. Therefore, we ought
not expect to see in our lifetime anyone who can

"heal the sick, raise the dead, cleanse lepers, cast out demons." Such signs were authorized by God for a certain purpose in a certain historical era.

Some may want to argue that the Twelve got all the meat and potatoes, leaving us with pretty thin gravy! The sacraments seem a very poor shadow of raising the dead, restoring lepers, and exorcising demons. Are we then to substitute symbols for direct active intervention on behalf of the dying, the diseased, the possessed? In the place of miracles, rituals? In the place of saving acts, gestures?

If indeed the sacraments are seen as signs in the modern sense, as pointers or advertisements or indicators, then they are devoid of power. But what if we are to apprehend them as signs in the same sense that we apprehend Jesus' works of healing and resurrection as signs? What if Baptism and the Supper are inseparable from the announcement that the kingdom of God is at hand? Then they are not merely signs that can be replaced with other indicators; they may be indeed those extraordinary labors we are called to perform, as surely as the Twelve were called to raise the dead and cast out demons.

But have we just performed a magic trick? We began with Christ's call to go hand to hand with humankind's ancient foes and ended up with . . . ecclesiastical rituals! Talk about a shell game! The pea was visible, but the magician made it disappear. And when it appeared, it had been turned into something else! But are the sacraments of Baptism and the Supper such a far cry from what the Twelve were authorized by Jesus to perform? For what do Baptism and the Supper signify—show forth for all to see—if not the minis-

try of Jesus Christ to a diseased, demon-ridden,
dying humanity? Paul could speak of Christians
as being "buried therefore with [Christ] by baptism into death, so that as Christ was raised from
the dead by the glory of the Father, we too might
walk in newness of life" (Rom. 6:4). Baptism is a
sign of cleansing and restoration. In Jesus' time
lepers were outcasts, unclean persons who needed
to be cleansed to be reincorporated into the people
of God. In Christian understanding, Baptism is
not only a washing with water; it is our anointing
with the Spirit of God, in which God's Spirit comes
into our lives to replace or displace other spirits.
And the Supper is a showing forth of Christ's
death until he comes again, a foretaste of eating
and drinking in the kingdom, where death and
disease and evil have been banished once and for
all.

Extraordinary Labors

Some may be moved by this interpretation of
Matthew 9:35–10:8a to wonder out loud, If that is
true, ho hum! The priests have once more gained
the upper hand; it is only what the priests do in
the sanctuary that really matters; nothing in the
world outside has changed; people go on getting
sick and dying and fighting with drugs and alcohol
possession and being shunned for various forms of
uncleanness. But not to worry! The church cele-
brates the sacraments. And it is marvelous in
God's eyes.

That is a fair comment and deserves a response.
Note that Matthew indicates that the marvelous
works were given to the whole church. That is

what the Twelve represent. It is the whole church that carries on the ministry of Jesus, not just an ordained priesthood. If the sacraments seem to have no power, could it be because they have been given over by us to a priestly class—and have become signs of the power of those priests rather than signs of the power of God over death, disease, and the devil?

If we see the sacraments as mere rituals, is that not a failure of the church to keep word and sign together? It would seem from our interpretation of Matthew 9:35–10:8a that the two are not to be separated, that they become powerless if disjoined. There is no way to prove, historically, that where the church has been equally vigorous in preaching the word and celebrating the sacraments, there Christ has been powerfully present, demonstrating his victory over death, disease, and evil. But that is not the argument of this chapter. The argument of this chapter is that the extraordinary labors to which Christ calls his church today may well be the celebration of the sacraments of Baptism and the Supper, joined to the bold proclamation of his sovereignty over all the powers that threaten the welfare of humankind.

The King's Commendation

We might prefer that Christ called us to labors more heroic than those suggested here. But I am reminded of a favorite story from childhood. Once there was a young page who served in a king's castle. Each day the knights went forth to battle with the powers of evil; and each evening they came home, weary and wounded. And he who fought most bravely would have a special reward: On his shield would shine a supernaturally lighted cross!

One day, when the forces of evil were most threatening, the page was left alone to guard the castle, with strict instructions to let down the drawbridge for no one. During the day several came and begged admittance: a poor woman with a sick child, a beggar, a wounded knight. But the little page clung to his promise, for evil was known to wear various disguises. At the end of the day, when the knights came home battered but victorious, the king was amazed to discover that the shield of the page was the one that bore the shining cross!

You and I, like the boy in the tale, are called to duties that may not seem at all extraordinary. Off in the distance we hear the sounds of battle, where others are engaged in hand-to-hand warfare with the legions of evil. But we have our tasks. They are not always easy. Yet we too may hope for a victor's reward and the King's commendation.

6

*The Call
to Extend the Family*

*While [Jesus] was still speaking to the people, be-
hold, his mother and brothers stood outside, asking to speak to him. But he replied to the man who
told him, "Who is my mother, and who are my
brothers?" And stretching out his hand toward his
disciples, he said, "Here are my mother and my
brothers! For whoever does the will of my Father in
heaven is my brother, and sister, and mother."*
                              —Matthew 12:46–50

Jesus ducked a meeting with his mother and
brothers; he said that his disciples were mother
and brother enough for him. In resisting the
claims of his relatives, he illustrated a contemporary quandary of ours. In designating his disciples
as his extended family, he provided us with a solution to that quandary. The quandary may be
stated as a question: Who is my true family? The
solution may be stated as follows: In family matters, our Christian calling is to be loyal to the
extended family of the faithful.

Many people today share nagging life concerns:
Who am I? Where did I come from? The questions
are not asked by adopted children only; they have

become the questions of the larger society. In a mobile, rapidly changing, always moving culture, it isn't easy to keep a firm grasp on one's identity. Identity crises are as catching as the common cold! And so the question, Who is my real family? becomes more than curiosity about one's genealogy.

When we have read the incident in Matthew 12:46–50, questions linger in our own minds: Who is *my* true family? Who has claim to the time, attention, energy, money, and prayers that naturally belong to my blood relatives—the father who sired me, the mother who nursed me, the brothers and sisters who share the same genes? Many come in the guise of mother and sister and brother, demanding that we turn aside from what we are doing and honor their demands. Not just two or three people clutch at our sleeves and claim the rights of mother and siblings; there is a host of them! Sects, tribes, churches, states, corporations, cultures, classes—each ask that we recognize a bond that is as strong as blood. In no particular order of priority or importance, they are as follows:

There are those groups that for want of a better name we call sects or cults: They are what Eric Hoffer calls "true believers," who would meld us into themselves in a bonding as intimate and permanent as the biological family. The Moonies— members of the Unification Church—are such a group, and they have many counterparts that have not earned the Moonies' questionable reputation. The great appeal of true believers is that they offer to be our surrogate family. They promise—particularly to the young adult—more than the grudging acceptance based on duty and blood of the natural family. Home with them is more than Robert Frost's "place where, when you have to go there they have to take you in." They offer the warmth and intimacy that many recall knowing as infants with their mothers; they offer the authority and value strength many can remember honoring in their fathers. And to the young adult they offer these things at the same time that they offer a chance to leave the nest and make a break with the biological family. In *Habits of the Heart* the authors say of our American culture, "However painful the process of leaving home, for parents and for children, the really frightening thing for both would be the prospect of the child never leaving home." The sect or cult offers a double benefit: You can leave home without giving up family; we will be your family.

The church, as represented in the mainline denominations, makes a similar offer to the individual, although mainline churches are in the front ranks of those who despise and fear the cults. In the rhetoric of the churches are considerable references to the Christian fellowship as family. Congregational programs are shot through with references to "our church family." It is certainly no accident that the titles of Father, Brother, and Sister have found their way into ecclesiastical language. If you asked a sampling of church members to pick one metaphor to describe their relationship to a congregation, you would find many using the term "family." And if you asked the average church member what he or she wished his or her congregation to be more like, it would again be the family metaphor that would come forth.

This use of the metaphor of the family to desig-
nate the church gets support from theologians.
John P. Meier writes (p. 140), "For [Matthew] the
church is the family of God, incorporated into the
communal life of the Godhead through baptism."

The list of groups claiming to be one's true family is a long one, and no great purpose is served by
being exhaustive. But the following claimants deserve some mention, however brief. The race or
tribe makes its claim; "we white folks," "we black
folks," are phrases used to command loyalty, as
though racial bonds had a right to demand alle-
giance similar to those of the biological family.

While the nation-state does not claim to be our
extended family, it often lays claim to the family
as one of its essential building blocks. The subtle
suggestion is that the family finds its reason for
being in the larger entity. National leaders are
prone to appeal to the family as essential to the
well-being of the nation. In his commencement
speech at Howard University in 1965, Lyndon
Johnson said, "The family is the cornerstone of
our society. More than any other force it shapes
the attitudes, the hopes, the ambitions, and the
values of the child." In his State of the Union
message in 1985, Ronald Reagan proclaimed, "As
the family goes, so goes our civilization."

Then also there is the claim of the corporation—
broadly understood as any body that supplies us
with a workplace, a work life, and income. This
may be a literal corporation, such as IBM or GE;
or it may be a body like the CIO or AFL, the pres-
bytery, the board of education, the Department of
Defense, the state legislature, Lincoln High
School, the Pittsburgh Pirates, or the Second Pla-

toon. For his book *The Good War,* Studs Terkel interviewed a number of World War II infantrymen. They said they fought not so much for honor or cause or even country as they did for their buddies; not to let the guys down—that was the most important thing in their lives as soldiers. Many confessed that when they got home their feelings of loyalty to spouses and parents were never as strong as their feelings for their fellows in the Second Platoon.

A Familiar Tug-of-War

Most of us have known what it is to be pulled in opposite directions by those claiming to be our family. Whether one is caught in a tug-of-war between a religious sect and one's parents, between the demands of the workplace and the claims of wife and children, or between the love of fellow soldiers and the love of wife and parents, the strains are very real. We can empathize with the dilemma faced by Jesus in the incident described in Matthew. He was at work in the company of friends when his mother and brothers came and asserted a claim to his attention. He was caught between legitimate demands. The Fifth Commandment, "Honor your father and your mother," could not be shrugged off; neither could the command to love your neighbor, represented by the people Jesus was teaching. The dilemma is real; the solution is anything but simple.

The problem of family loyalty is compounded in our generation by the breakup—some would call it the breakdown—of traditional family values. The question, Who is my family? has another question that gets asked alongside it: *What* is a family? The traditional notion that a family consists of a father and a mother and one or more children is under serious attack. Single women argue both for their right to have children outside of marriage and their right to raise children with no father on the scene. In the winter of 1987 a nurse from Madison, Wisconsin, was interviewed on television. A single woman in her thirties, she intended to be impregnated by a friend in order that she might have a child, whom she intended to raise by herself.

This woman may not be dismissed as pathetically mistaken. Writing in *God's Fierce Whimsy,* a group of feminine theologians said, "We celebrate also the possibility for which we struggle: that someday *all* of us—and our sisters, daughters, granddaughters, god-daughters, namesakes, and nieces—will inhabit a world in which motherhood is fully and freely a gift and an option, available to all who desire it, whether married or single, lesbian or straight." This is in defiance not only of conventional Christian and American values but of what anthropologist Bronislaw Malinowski called "the principle of legitimacy." All cultures, he said, insist that every child shall have a recognized father. "The most important moral and legal rule concerning the physiological side of kinship," he wrote in *Sex, Culture, and Myth,* "is that no child should be brought into the world without a man—and one man at that—assuming the role of sociological father, that is, guardian and protector, the male link between the child and the rest of the community."

It is this clash between the lived experience of the human race and the values of modern radicals that made the Baby M case of 1987 such a national sensation. A woman agreed to be impregnated by the semen of the husband of another woman and to bear a child for that couple. After the baby was born, the surrogate mother could not bear to surrender the baby as promised. The case went to court and had most of America talking about it for several weeks.

We should not have been so taken by surprise. This happened in a country where in 1979, at a White House Conference on the Family, participants could not agree as to whether or not there is a societal norm that could be described simply as the American Family. Is it any wonder, then, that large numbers of persons in our society ask in all seriousness, Who is my true family? When Jesus said, "Who is my mother, and who are my brothers?" he spoke for all of us.

The Solution

However, the text in Matthew offers a solution as well as illustrating a problem. Jesus pointed to his disciples and said, "Here are my mother and my brothers! For whoever does the will of my Father in heaven is my brother, and sister, and mother." Both sentences are important. With the first Jesus set aside the claim of his mother and siblings to have first call on his time and efforts. He waved his hand at his friends and associates and named them his mother and brothers. With that one wave of his hand, Jesus relativized the

claims of his biological and social family. When in
the whole history of the world has one wave of the
hand wiped out so many millennia of custom?

The second sentence is equally important:
"Whoever does the will of my Father in heaven is
my brother, and sister, and mother." "The disciples . . . constitute the real family of Jesus . . . by
reason of the fact that they do God's will" (Hill, p.
222). Since it is doing God's will that makes one a
member of Jesus' family, it seems right to broaden
the concept of true family to include *all* who do
God's will, so that Jesus' disciples represent the
whole company of the faithful—past, present, and
future. It is to this great company that Jesus owes
family loyalty. It is to them he appeals for freedom
from the immediate demands of blood kinship.

"Whoever does the will of my Father in heaven"
is a tent under which a large company may be
assembled. Who, in biblical terms, has a right to
be under that tent? Abraham and Sarah, Isaac
and Rebekah, Jacob and Rachel, surely; if the pa-
triarchs and matriarchs don't belong there, who
does? Also under the canopy belong the prophets
who spoke Yahweh's word: Samuel, Huldah,
Amos. And surely David, who was a king after
God's heart. We would also want to name the
faithful listed in the New Testament: Mary, Peter,
and Paul. Nor would we want to omit from our list
those whom we name as our forebears in the
church: Augustine, Aquinas, Catherine, Theresa,
Calvin, Luther, Witherspoon, Knox. We all need
to make our own lists; any attempt to make a
complete one will surely leave out some who ought
to be there. When you make your roster, don't

forget such modern saints as Mother Teresa, Martin Luther King, Jr., and Dorothy Day.

When we are pressed to choose or value or take a stand on the basis of true family, it is this company of the faithful to whom we owe our loyalty. Their claim on us is stronger than the claim of our biological parents and siblings. It is their opinions and acceptance that we must value above all other group pressures or pulls.

The earliest Christian writing said to be by a woman is the diary of Perpetua, a citizen of Carthage. With others who refused to worship the Roman emperor, she was imprisoned during the persecutions of A.D. 202–203. She refused to heed the pleas of her father, who visited her in prison and urged her to compromise her stand. She gave up to her father her newborn son, whom she had been nursing in prison, choosing to surrender her role as mother rather than submit. In her diary she describes her appearance before the governor: "[He] said, 'Have pity on your father's grey head; have pity on your infant son; offer sacrifice for the emperor's welfare.' But I answered, 'I will not.' Hilarion asked, 'Are you a Christian?' And I answered, 'I am a Christian.' " Our Christian calling is to listen for voices like that of Perpetua and be faithful to them.

There is a corollary to this. In family matters our loyalty can never be to ourselves, to our individual self-interest, to conscience, or even to God alone. That is a modern heresy that has deluded millions into rebellion or submission. Our culture insists that adolescents learn to define themselves over and against their parents. We teach young

people that they are to throw off the parental yoke
and assert their individuality. Sometimes this cultural demand gets translated into a moral demand
and is given religious sanction. But in the terms of
what we have learned from Matthew 12:46–50, the
choice is never between the family and me; it is
always, in family matters, *between families*. The
question in family matters is never: Shall I be
loyal to the family or to myself? It is always: Who
is my true family? And the scriptural answer is:
Your true family is the company of the faithful,
the saints with whom you have communion.

Honor Your Father and Your Mother

To be loyal to the company of the faithful is
truly to honor father and mother in obedience to
the Fifth Commandment. It is not an evasion of
that command; it is a fulfillment of it. It is a recognition that we have a "Father in heaven"—to use
Jesus' metaphor—from whom we learn who is our
true mother and who are our true brothers and
sisters.

This is admittedly a radical, not to say revolutionary, interpretation of the Fifth Commandment. In Jesus' culture, as in most cultures of the
world from the earliest days until the present, to
honor one's parents meant to obey them; to put
their welfare and their values and their wishes
above one's own. To suggest that another group
had a prior claim on one's honoring was surely a
radical break with tradition. But that seems the
clear teaching of the passage from Matthew. John
Meier writes (p. 140), "The disciples, who have left
their own families for Jesus (8:22; 10:37) are his

real mother and brothers. What Jesus asked of his disciples—the breaking of family ties—he himself now undertakes."

In practical terms, of course, honoring the company of the faithful and obeying one's earthly parents and siblings is often one and the same thing. For who has taught us to know the faithful if not our family? Where did we learn the stories of Abraham and Sarah if not at our mother's knee? And would we indeed claim Jesus as Sovereign if our fathers had not done the same? We need to be careful not to set up a false rivalry between natural family and the company of the faithful when, in fact, such a rivalry does not often exist.

But sometimes such a rivalry does exist, and it is surely one of the most painful of all human dilemmas. When I was eighteen, I had a college friend who was the most committed Christian I had ever met. When I visited his suburban home, I was shocked to find that he and his father were at serious odds. His father, a faithful church member and a good citizen and a hard worker, could not understand his son's passion for God's kingdom. He thought his son's decision to be a minister was a waste of time and money, not to mention the young man's commitment to pacifism and socialism. When I heard my friend try to defend himself against his father, I heard echoes of the young Jesus in the temple, saying to his upset parents, "Did you not know that I must be in my Father's house?" (Luke 2:49).

One of the most poignant experiences for young people growing up in our society is to espouse some cause such as civil rights or world peace—a cause they learned to love in their home or church—and then find that their parents are opposed to overt action on behalf of social justice. It is at best bittersweet to be forced to say to one's own parents, "Who is my mother, and who are my brothers? . . . Whoever does the will of my Father in heaven is my brother, and sister, and mother."

In English literature there are three classic family matters in which persons are pressed to choose between loyalty to biological family and loyalty to some other group or norm. We have already illustrated the tug-of-war between the parent and the child who is bent on a vocational course that the parent doesn't like. That conflict is brilliantly delineated in C. P. Snow's novel, *The Conscience of the Rich*. The protagonists are Charles March and his father. The Marches are a wealthy family living in London in the times between the two wars. Charles, largely to please his father, launches a career as a trial lawyer, but suddenly he throws that over and starts the study of medicine. His father is outraged; he understands the decision for what it is, an act of independence. He is never reconciled to Charles's new occupation. He uses an ancient Japanese phrase to describe the feeling caused by the rupture between him and his son, "the darkness of the heart."

Another classic dilemma is that of the parent who cannot let the child become independent. In a series of novels about life in a small town in Canada, Robertson Davies tells of the plight of Solomon Bridgetower, who is tyrannized by his invalid mother. She insists that he live with her and abide by her wishes about girlfriends and all sorts of things. When she dies, she leaves her fortune tied up in such a way that Solly has to wait for years to have free use of the money. From beyond the grave her long hand reaches back to jerk him around. We can all tell stories about such relationships, in which the mother—or some other close relative—used blood ties as slave bracelets.

In counseling with young persons, I often found them torn between the need to be free and the need to obey. It was not that they lacked courage to rebel. (It does not seem to me that it takes courage to rebel, only a kind of willful need to self-destruct.) What they most desperately needed was a third option—an alternative to submission or rebellion, both of which they wisely understood to be acts of folly.

The third classic dilemma—called classic because it appears over and over again in literature and drama—is the tug-of-war between love for one's family and love for an alien. In *Fiddler on the Roof* the Jewish Tevye is able to tolerate his first daughter's marriage to a poor tailor. He is able to reconcile himself to his second daughter's marrying a radical student. But he casts away his third daughter for falling in love with a Russian Gentile. In his world, there can be no kinship between Gentile and Jew.

Let us return to what our Gospel text says about such family matters. The teaching of Matthew 12: 46–50 may be summarized as follows: *In family matters our loyalty as Christians belongs to the company of the faithful.* That is our calling. We are never to suppose that we owe absolute loyalty to any social, racial, or religious group. Nor are we to claim independence from all groups on the grounds that we have some kind of divine right to be autonomous. Rather, we are to honor our mothers and fathers and brothers and sisters in the faith. Surely this is what the writer of Hebrews intended when he wrote, "Therefore, since we are surrounded by so great a cloud of witnesses, let us also lay aside every weight, and sin which clings so closely, and let us run with perseverance the race that is set before us" (Heb. 12:1).

7

The Call to Costly Obedience

Then Jesus told his disciples, "If any man would come after me, let him deny himself and take up his cross and follow me. For whoever would save his life will lose it, and whoever loses his life for my sake will find it. For what will it profit a man, if he gains the whole world and forfeits his life? Or what shall a man give in return for his life? For the Son of man is to come with his angels in the glory of his Father, and then he will repay every man for what he has done. Truly, I say to you, there are some standing here who will not taste death before they see the Son of man coming in his kingdom."
—Matthew 16:24–28

By his works and words Jesus blazed a perilous path for others to follow. He determined to go to the capital city of Jerusalem at a time when public humiliation and execution were high probabilities. Over him, as he went, hung the shadow of the cross. In his day the cross represented what the gallows, the firing squad, or the electric chair represents to us. And he said to Peter and others who would be his disciples, "If any man would

come after me, let him . . . take up his cross and
follow me."

Jesus calls us to costly obedience. Discipleship
comes with a price tag shaped in the form of a
cross. To follow him is to set foot on that blazed
trail that leads to the city where the powers of
destruction are lodged.

Where that trail forks off from the main road,
there is a well-worn sign; it reads *Prophetic Alternative.* We have said Jesus blazed a trail; it might
be more accurate to say he reopened a trail that
had been closed for a long, long time. For the way
of costly obedience was once well known in Israel;
it was known to Moses, Samuel, and Isaiah. The
trail is called prophetic because of its linkages to
those great prophets; it is called an alternative
because it offers a clear choice. It leads away from
another path laid down in scripture.

Prudential Morality

The broad highway from which the trail
branches off is the *Path of Prudential Morality.* It
was also well known in Israel. It is the way of life
most fully described by the book of Deuteronomy,
by many of the Psalms, and by the Wisdom literature. It comes in full and direct expression in
Psalm 1 (vs. 1–3):

> Blessed is the man
>   who walks not in the counsel of the wicked,
> nor stands in the way of sinners,
>   nor sits in the seat of scoffers;
> but his delight is in the law of the LORD,
>   and on his law he meditates day and night.

> He is like a tree
>   planted by streams of water,
> that yields its fruit in its season,
>   and its leaf does not wither.
> In all that he does, he prospers.

According to the author of this psalm, God is a rock upon which to build a secure, long, and productive life. Do you wish to be healthy? Live long? Have many grandchildren? Enjoy the best the world has to offer? Go to your grave in peace? Then obey the law of God; seek those affairs that make for law and order and peace and honor among men. Along the Path of Prudential Morality are signs that promise: Take care to obey God's law and God will take care of you. Like a drumbeat accompanying a melody, the words are sounded again and again in Deuteronomy: "Therefore you shall keep [God's] . . . commandments, . . . that it may go well with you, . . . and that you may prolong your days" (Deut. 4:40).

That point of view is well represented in the Bible. It comes to expression also in the Wisdom literature:

> Honor the LORD with your substance
>   and with the first fruits of all your produce;
> then your barns will be filled with plenty,
>   and your vats will be bursting with wine.
> —Proverbs 3:9–10

We all ought to be familiar with this path. It is one our generation has beaten smooth. It is represented in our day by liberal arts colleges, the Masons, Rotary, life insurance, Religion in American

Life, the Anti-Defamation League, the League
of Women Voters, Reader's Digest, the Jaycees,
the Pro-Choice Movement, Robert Schuller, the
WCTU, Common Cause, savings banks, the Moral
Majority, William Buckley, the Institute for Religion and Democracy—and many preachers of the
mainline denominations.

These institutions and individuals—and others
like them—represent what Reinhold Niebuhr
called "the nicely calculated more-or-less of prudential morality." For what is the basis of their
appeal to the average man and woman? They appeal to the instinct that is in all of us to opt for a
good life, for a better world, for the most pleasure
for the most people.

Writing of life in Amarillo, Texas, A. G. Moj-
tabai says in *Blessed Assurance* (pp. 100–101),
"The notion of some sort of quid pro quo between
prosperity and piety as an index—an outward and
visible sign of righteousness—is widespread and
long preexistent in Amarillo and the nation.
'God's dynamic laws of prosperity,' as Rev. Dick
Marcear, pastor of Amarillo's prospering Central
Church of Christ, likes to call them, have a dis-
tinctly contractual cast."

Pastor Marcear knows his scripture; prudential
morality is indeed biblical. One can appeal to the
Bible if one wants to make a case for this kind of
way of picturing the good—read "godly"—life.

Prophetic Alternative

However, there is another pathway laid out in
the Bible. It is a way of life that by no means
guarantees health, long life, prosperity, or even

happiness. It is the way of costly obedience. It is foreshadowed in the preaching of the prophets of Israel, most especially the Servant Songs of Isaiah. It comes to full expression in the cross of Jesus of Nazareth. However, there are a number of places in the life of Israel when there was a foreshadowing of Jesus' choice of the cross. Here are three of them.

When the people of Israel were suffering slavery and oppression in Egypt, God appeared to Moses in a burning bush and summoned him to go to Egypt to be a liberator. Moses rightly perceived the deadly danger of opposing the pharaoh, surely one of the most powerful rulers on earth. He tried desperately to avoid God's call. What prudent man puts his head in the mouth of a lion? And yet Moses went down into Egypt.

When the children of Israel were wandering in the desert, many of them grumbled against the foolishness that brought them there. They remembered fondly the melons and leeks eaten in Egypt. Fruits and vegetables enjoyed in bondage seemed better than hungering as free men and women in the Sinai desert! Their leader, Moses, held out only a wilderness journey with a promise that somewhere up ahead for some of them, someday, there would be a Promised Land. To follow the vision of Moses—which led through a dry and thorny desert—or to return over a well-beaten path to the melons and leeks of Egypt—these were the alternatives open to them. It is hard to see how a prudent man or woman would not turn back to Egypt. And yet they turned their backs to Egypt and went on.

When those Israelites who survived forty years

of wilderness wandering had finally settled in the
Promised Land, they found it no Garden of Eden.
They were continually harassed by stronger, bet-
ter-armed tribes. In desperation, the elders went
to the prophet Samuel and asked for a king, such
as other people had. A king, they reasoned, could
organize a defense against their enemies. It was
prudential morality of the highest sort. Who does
not have a right to defend himself or herself
against lawless elements? And yet Samuel tried to
dissuade them, pointing out that God was their
king; God would protect them. Furthermore, an
Israelite king would conscript their sons into the
army and make servants of their daughters and
raise their taxes. But being prudent men and
knowing that there is a price to be paid for freedom, they did not listen to Samuel; they insisted
on a king. This was a choice with fateful conse-
quences; it was the monarchy that proved their
downfall.

The richest metaphors of the Prophetic Alternative are in the book of Isaiah. This prophet and
those associated with him saw that the call of God
to Israel was not to recover the glory of kings
David and Solomon but to be a Suffering Servant
among the nations. Not prosperity and long life
was God's way for Israel, but suffering for righteousness' sake, a nation rejected and despised by
the rulers of this world.

> For he grew up before him like a young plant,
>   and like a root out of dry ground;
> he had no form or comeliness that we should
>   look at him,
>   and no beauty that we should desire him.

He was despised and rejected by men;
  a man of sorrows, and acquainted with grief;
and as one from whom men hide their faces
he was despised, and we esteemed him not.
                       —Isaiah 53:2–3

The Prophetic Alternative comes to full expression in the ministry and example of Jesus. The most explicit statement of it is Matthew 16:24–28, where Jesus warns that anyone who follows him must risk crucifixion. "To 'lose one's life for Jesus' sake' means to risk life, to the point of death, in order obediently to witness to Jesus and his gospel" (Hill, p. 265).

The trouble with the Prophetic Alternative, as Jesus pointed out to his disciples, is that it is imprudent. It is fraught with risk. It most assuredly involves one in suffering, in a clash with the principalities that "bear the sword" (Rom. 13:4), with those "rulers of this age . . . [who] crucified the Lord of glory" (1 Cor. 2:8). The cross that Jesus invites his disciples to shoulder is a literal cross; it is the public rejection and torture and death that await those who take up, with Jesus, the cause of God's righteous rule in the earth!

If you chose this alternative, which is to stand with Jesus for God's righteous rule in this world and against all those principalities and powers that perpetuate injustice, you gamble everything dear. You chose a risky path, one that will lead most certainly near, if not to, what the cross represented for Jesus: rejection, public humiliation, and death. Ask Martin Luther King, Jr., who said from Reidsville State Prison in Georgia, "This is the cross that we must bear for the freedom of our

people." Ask Dietrich Bonhoeffer, who was imprisoned for his part in the plot to overthrow Adolf
Hitler; he wrote of "costly grace." Ask Allan
Boesak of South Africa, outspoken foe of apartheid, whose life is daily at risk. He writes in *Comfort and Protest,* "In order for Christ to reconcile
the world with God, he had to die on the cross.
What makes us think we will get away with less?"
Ask Dom Helder Câmara, Brazilian bishop and
leader of the nonviolent movement for democracy
in Latin America. He said, "We shall not walk on
roses, people will not throng to hear us and ap-
plaud, and we shall not always be aware of divine
protection. If we are to be pilgrims for justice and
peace, we must expect the desert." Ask any mar-
tyr of our day or other days. They will tell you of
the terror of inviting the wrath of those earthly
rulers who have the power to imprison and execute.

What each of those just named had to forsake in
obedience to Christ is Prudential Morality, the
attempt through careful choices of good over evil
to secure their lives and their place in God's favor.
And that is just the choice that Jesus presents to
all who would be his disciples—to leave the broad
and well-traveled way for the difficult and narrow
way of costly obedience. His call to costly discipleship does not come to people who are playing
bridge or drinking beer in a tavern or potting
flowers or are otherwise pleasantly engaged. His
call to take up the cross comes to those who are
busy trying to secure their lives against the threat
of death and meaninglessness.

A Great Reversal

What we have in Matthew 16:25 is a Great Reversal: "For whoever would save his life will lose it, and whoever loses his life for my sake will find it." Where is the reversal? The normal perception of the godly life is of persons taking thought for doing good in order that they may prosper. Do you recall the question put to Jesus by the rich young man? "Teacher, what good deed must I do, to have eternal life?" One could write a history of the world's religions in terms of that question and the various answers people have given to it. Jesus' answer is the one of costly obedience: "Go, sell what you possess and give to the poor, and you will have treasure in heaven; and come, follow me."

What Jesus offered to the rich young man, whose feet were firmly fixed on the path of Prudential Morality, was the Prophetic Alternative. Jesus said, in effect: If you continue to try to secure the favor of God through good works and the like you will not secure your life, you will lose it; that path leads to extinction. If you really want to find or secure your life, follow me. Seek God's kingdom. Join the movement for God's peace and justice—and God will give you eternal life as a gift!

What Jesus offered for the young man's consideration was another form of the appeal of the apostle Paul to faith rather than works: If you seek through good works to secure the favor of God, you only condemn yourself; the law becomes an implacable judge. But if you throw yourself on the mercy of God in Christ, you are born again into a new existence.

But we must not get too far away from Jesus'
words, "Take up [the] cross and follow me." He
called the disciples to commit themselves to his
kingdom enterprise at the risk of being crushed by
the powers that be. In Jesus' time, that risk was
properly and graphically represented by a wooden
cross. "It was an Oriental form of torture and
death, adopted by Rome for slaves and rebels, but
not for Roman citizens. By holding before his disciples the most horrifying and shameful type of
death, Jesus stresses that no sacrifice can be too
great simply to 'follow me' " (Meier, p. 114).

What is a proper and graphic representation in
our generation for the cross? Falling into the clut-
ches of a Central American death squad? Impris-
onment? Solitary confinement? A firing squad?
Torture in a "dirty war"? A Korean friend of mine
was given the airplane torture by the Japanese
during World War II. In an effort to get him to
deny his Christian faith, they stood him on a table,
tied his arms behind his back with a rope hanging
from the ceiling, and then kicked the table away.
I have an Indonesian friend whose Presbyterian
minister father was imprisoned and shot by the
Japanese during World War II as an enemy of the
state.

I cite those examples, not to point the finger at
any particular government but to demonstrate
that taking up the cross is not something limited
to the first century. It is required of Christians in
every generation.

There is a sense in which all Christians are
called to demonstrate their willingness to deny
themselves and take up the cross. We call the

Lord's Supper a sacrament. The word "sacrament" comes from a Latin word that was used for the oath of loyalty that a Roman soldier took to the emperor. A soldier took a *sacramentum* to serve the emperor faithfully, even unto death. In a similar way, when we drink the cup and eat the bread of the Supper, are we not "remembering the Lord's death" until he comes again? Are we not testifying that his kind of life leads to death on the cross? Are we not renewing our vows to be faithful to him until death?

It seems altogether fitting that one of the Christian martyrs of our time, Archbishop Oscar Romero, received a bullet in the heart just as he was about to pronounce these words of the Mass from behind the altar of the Chapel of the Divine Providence in San Salvador: "This is my body given for you."

It cannot be said often enough that the cross in Jesus' call is a literal cross; it is public execution. Dietrich Bonhoeffer was hanged for his participation with other Christians in the plot to assassinate Hitler and end the Nazi terror. Those who resist apartheid in South Africa feel the full force of the state, with its power to imprison and execute. It is that "cross" that is meant in Jesus' call—not just any suffering that happens to befall Christians, like ulcers, a bad marriage, or death on the highway at the hands of a drunken driver.

The first martyrs of the Christian church in Uganda were young pages at the court of the king. When they were about to be burned alive for their faith, each was asked to name the charge against

him. Each said, "For following Christ." They understood what Jesus meant when he said, "If any
man would come after me, let him deny himself
and take up his cross and follow me."

Taking up the cross has become widely used to
describe all manner of human difficulties. "Time
on the cross" is what some call service in the
British governance of Northern Ireland. Sometimes Christians, in trying to find meaning in a
physical handicap or a loss of income, will say,
"That's just my cross; I'll have to bear it." One
needs to say gently to such folk, "No. That is not
your cross. It may be a thorn in the side, but it is
not a cross."

We must not allow the cross of Jesus to be de-
valued, to be privatized by such talk. Jesus did not
die in a plane crash, or by catching a fatal disease,
or from cancer, or in a fall off a mountain. He was
put to death by the combined will of the religious
authorities, the populace, and the forces of law
and order—what the Bible calls "principalities
and powers." And to follow Jesus, to become part
of his movement for peace and righteousness,
means to risk the wrath of those principalities,
who have it within their power to do to us what
they did to Jesus. "As goes the Master, so goes the
disciple" (Meier, p. 187).

Even if we were strongly inclined to understand
"take up his cross" to refer to shouldering some
personal deprivation or disability, the text of Matthew would not allow it. For appended to the call
to cross-bearing is this warning: "For the Son of
man is to come with his angels in the glory of his
Father, and then he will repay every man for what

he has done. Truly, I say to you, there are some standing here who will not taste death before they see the Son of man coming in his kingdom" (Matt. 16:27–28).

The "Son of man," whom Christians understand to be Jesus in his risen power and status, is clearly both a ruler and a judge. "The reason why disciples must follow in the way of sacrificial living is that there is a coming judgement" (Hill, p. 265). In the Old Testament a judge was not so much someone who handed out sentences as one who judged between parties to set things right. When the Son of man comes, he will put things right; he will establish the kingdom of peace and righteousness that is promised in the prophetic literature of the Old Testament. The Son of man will judge the judges of this world and overrule the rulers; he is clearly a political as well as a religious figure. It is in behalf of this Jesus that we are called to "take up the cross," which rather clearly cannot mean anything but what we have understood it to mean in this chapter. It is to risk danger and death at the hands of the judges and rulers of this world.

This is one of the most difficult concepts in scripture for Americans to understand. We find it hard to get it into our heads and hearts that "government of the people, by the people, and for the people" might act against the cause of Christ, might subvert peace and justice, might put national security ahead of justice. We still have not learned the lesson of Vietnam; democratic governments are not necessarily more moral than oligarchies or totalitarian governments; they are capable of cruel self-deception. They are, as M.

Scott Peck describes in *People of the Lie,* capable
of evil.

Several questions hang in the air, begging for
answers. One has to do with world-denying religions like Buddhism. They call upon adherents to
give up the attempt to live according to desires
and appetites and pleasures—to save the soul by
denying the body. Isn't that a possible meaning of
"take up his cross"? Or at least of "deny himself"?
Not in a Christian context. We believe that God
made the world good, that God wills goodness and
life for humankind. To deny ourselves in that
sense would be a denial of the very God in whom
we believe.

The other question that hangs in the air is this:
Why should anyone be crazy enough to take such
a risky path? Why not take one's chances with the
Path of Prudential Morality, trusting that God
will reward good and decent behavior? Ah! But
Jesus' promise is that the Son of man, when he
comes as God's judge, will not look upon things
that way. When the judge comes—who is also the
crucified one—he will ask, Why did you try to secure your own life through good works, when I
paid the price of my life to secure yours? Was it for
nothing that I died for you? Could I have done it
by being reasonable? Moral? Decent? Kindly? *If at
the heart of God there is a cross, there must be a
cross in the heart of those who would love and
serve God. Think about that—the rest of your life.*

The message of Jesus' cross is clearly this: One
died and suffered for all; no one need pay for his
or her sins; misery in this life is not punishment
for wrongdoing. And the reverse is equally true:
There is no promise that if we suffer patiently and

cheerfully from our disabilities or accidents, God will reward us. Such sufferings are a part of our lot as humans. The question Jesus puts to each of us is not, Will you accept cheerfully and patiently whatever suffering life brings you? Rather, it is, Will you heed my call to work for justice and peace, even if that brings you into conflict with the judges and rulers of this world, who have the power to put you to death?

Let us take as our model for Christian discipleship Edith Stein. She was a German Jew who was converted to Christianity and became a Roman Catholic nun. When World War II came, she was hunted down by the Nazis and taken to a concentration camp—Auschwitz—where, until she was gassed, she busied herself with comforting and consoling the other internees. Edith Stein reminds us both of the demand of Christ and of the awful face of the state when it pretends to act in the national interest.

Edith Stein was a Carmelite nun. Lest we think all martyrdom is at the hand of right-wing states, we do well to remember the fate of those nuns whose death at the hands of the French Revolution is chronicled by Poulenc in his opera *Dialogues of the Carmelites.* In the final scene of the opera the small band of nuns is on stage, singing the praises of Christ. One by one they are led to the guillotine, which is offstage. The audience hears the awful *whomp* of the blade—and one less singer. Finally there is a single nun, who goes swiftly and gladly, still singing, to her fate. The opera is based on history; there was a convent of nuns who were executed by the leftist revolution for being enemies of the people.

Each Generation

To each generation the call to take up the cross comes in a different way. It is much easier to look back with hindsight to other generations and their call than it is to hear Christ's call in our day.

In the PBS version of *Goodbye, Mr. Chips,* in the year 1916 a student chooses to go to prison rather than serve in a war he has come to believe is wrong. He does this in defiance even of the saintly Chips, whom he dearly loves.

In 1934 the Confessing Church in Germany took a stand against Hitler when the majority of Christians supported his new regime.

When as a child I visited Korea in 1935, I heard the missionaries of the Presbyterian Church debating the so-called Shrine Controversy. The colonial overlords of Japan demanded that all Korean schoolchildren go to the Shinto shrines and bow to the emperor. Some missionaries saw that as idolatry; others thought it wise to do what the rulers asked and call it a patriotic gesture.

In the 1960s in the United States the early protesters against the war in Vietnam found their parents and pastors hostile to their views.

As we look back, it may seem to us rather easy to discern the will of Christ. However, it must have been extraordinarily difficult for those folks to make choices.

What are the issues and causes in the remainder of the twentieth century that call us to the cross? The Sanctuary movement? The struggle against Soviet imperialism? Resistance against our government's policy in Central America? Opposition to nuclear armaments? The fight against racism? The war on drugs? The struggle for gay rights? The battle for the environment? Whatever the issue, we may be sure of this: It will be costly. When the call comes, we must remember the words of Jesus: "For what does it profit a man, to gain the whole world and forfeit his life?"

8

The Call to Fidelity

And Pharisees came up to him and tested him by asking, "Is it lawful to divorce one's wife for any cause?" He answered, "Have you not read that he who made them from the beginning made them male and female, and said, 'For this reason a man shall leave his father and mother and be joined to his wife, and the two shall become one flesh'? So they are no longer two but one flesh. What therefore God has joined together, let not man put asunder." They said to him, "Why then did Moses command one to give a certificate of divorce, and to put her away?" He said to them, "For your hardness of heart Moses allowed you to divorce your wives, but from the beginning it was not so. And I say to you: whoever divorces his wife, except for unchastity, and marries another, commits adultery."
—Matthew 19:3–9

Sexual fidelity in marriage, that is the calling of Christians. Those who are now married are summoned by Christ to remain faithful to their partners until death should part them. The glue that holds Christian spouses together is not romantic love, nor is it law. It is loyalty—lifelong fidelity.

That will come as a surprise—perhaps a nasty shock—to those who suppose that we are living through a sexual revolution in which adultery has become as irrelevant as the buggy whip. They are looking for a new definition of Christian marriage that will allow for premarital sex, divorce, serial monogamy, and victimless extramarital affairs. It is true that we are living through a sexual crisis. Divorce among clergy is commonplace; church members cohabit before marriage; Christian spouses espouse open marriage. But if we listen obediently to Matthew's Gospel, we must name it a crisis and not a revolution. Christ calls us to return to the once commonly accepted notion that marriage is for life and that adultery is proscribed by the Seventh Commandment.

To those who find the present crisis in sexual morality upsetting, it may be a comfort to learn that things were not much different in Jesus' own time. The confrontation between Jesus and some Pharisees, reported in Matthew 19:3–9, reflects a struggle with sexual ethics. The Pharisees asked him, "Is it lawful to divorce one's wife for any cause?" Behind that question lay a bitter dispute. Followers of Rabbi Hillel held that the Law allowed a man to divorce his wife for almost anything that displeased him—burning the toast, a wart on her chin, growing obese—while the followers of Rabbi Shammai held that the offense must be serious, like committing adultery. Both schools appealed to Deuteronomy 24:1, which permitted a man to divorce his wife on account of "indecency." It was the "indecency" that was at issue between the followers of Hillel and Shammai. Some said it could be anything that dis-

pleased the husband; others said it could only be
unchastity or something equally heinous. Pharisees came to Jesus to put him to the test, to see
where his views lay.

Jesus sided with neither party. He reiterated a
stand previously taken in the Sermon on the
Mount; he rejected the legitimacy of divorce. In
the Sermon he admitted: "It was also said [in the
Torah], 'Whoever divorces his wife, let him give
her a certificate of divorce.' But I say to you that
every one who divorces his wife, except on the
ground of unchastity, makes her an adulteress;
and whoever marries a divorced woman commits
adultery" (Matt. 5:31–32). In his discussion with
the Pharisees, Jesus said pretty much the same
thing: "For your hardness of heart Moses allowed
you to divorce your wives. . . . I say to you: whoever
divorces his wife, except for unchastity, and marries another, commits adultery." It is widely recognized that the New Testament in general and
the Gospels in particular hold to a straightforward
rejection of divorce as acceptable for Christians.

Jesus grounded his objection to divorce in the
intention of the Creator. As a Supreme Court Justice might go behind years of accepted legal prece-
dents to appeal to the intentions of the framers of
the U.S. Constitution, so Jesus went behind the
teaching of Deuteronomy to the intent of God as
recorded in Genesis. "Have you not read that
[God] who made [human beings] from the beginning made them male and female, and said, 'For
this reason a man shall leave his father and
mother and be joined to his wife, and the two shall
become one flesh'?" It belongs to the created order

of things that men and women should be joined in sexual union; neither gender is complete without the other. God intended that each should find wholeness in union with the other. Marriage, thus understood, is a divine calling.

This insight into the intention of the Creator needs to be kept front and center in any discussions of sexuality. We hear lots of talk—and some of it in church circles—about women and men having to do certain things because of their physiological or psychological makeup. As though an objective observation of *how* sex functions would tell us *for what purpose* we were created sexual beings! If one reads magazines like *Playboy* and *Penthouse,* one gets the impression that sex is all behavior: A man has an organ; it fits into a woman's organ; therefore putting it there must be right since that is how the equipment functions. But if we follow Jesus' lead in reading Genesis, we understand that God made us male and female for something other than mere coupling. Train cars couple; human beings marry. "A man shall leave his father and mother and be joined to his wife, and the two shall become one flesh." Marriage is not something natural. In the natural world, one and one equals two. In marriage there is the possibility that two may become one!

The call of Christ is to discover the one flesh, the wholeness that happens when a woman and a man are joined. It is not that by nature a woman is incomplete without a man, and a man is incomplete without a woman. Each is summoned to discover something together that neither is capable of knowing separately. The individual happiness of each partner is not the goal of marriage; rather, that goal is unity.

In the movie *Children of a Lesser God* there is a stormy love affair between Sarah, deaf and mute, and James, a teacher at a school for the deaf. In the final scene, after a painful separation, James says to her, "Is there a place, not in silence and not in sound, where we can meet?" And she nods assent. That is the biblical promise of marriage, that there is a place—neither in maleness nor in femaleness, but somewhere in between—where a man and a woman can meet and be truly joined.

In confidence in that promise, Christians respond to the call to fidelity within the marriage relationship. They are willing to put aside thoughts of mere personal satisfaction, of escape, or of divorce. And to this call Christ appends a stern warning: "Whoever divorces his wife, except for unchastity, and marries another, commits adultery."

A Loophole?

There appears to be a loophole in Jesus' injunction against divorce—an escape clause, if you will. For he said, "Whoever divorces his wife, *except for unchastity,* and marries another, commits adultery" (emphasis added). As Jesus' teaching is presented in Matthew's Gospel, there is apparently a situation in which divorce is proper. In Mark's Gospel, in Luke's, and in Paul's writings divorce is rejected outright. But in Matthew's Gospel—both in the Sermon on the Mount and here in chapter 19—there is apparently an exception to the rule.

Divorce is permitted when a wife has proved unfaithful.

This famous exception has been used in the history of the church to countenance divorce. There was a time, not so long ago, when the law of the Presbyterian church forbade a pastor to hold office if he was divorced, unless he was the innocent party in an adultery. And there have been notorious cases where a husband or a wife deliberately committed adultery in order to obtain a divorce. Jesus would seem to have given back with one hand what he took away with the other. A tiny loophole proved to be a breach in the wall large enough to drive a truck through. For if divorce is permitted in some cases, why not in others? If it is not forbidden under any and all circumstances, why cannot any circumstances be interpreted as right for divorce?

There are a number of possible ways of interpreting the exception granted in Matthew 19:9. One can say with David Hill that Jesus upheld the dissolubility of marriage on the basis of Genesis, but that Jesus also permitted divorce in cases of adultery, which contravened the created order. Eduard Schweizer attributes the exception to the author of the Gospel, but says that it is "comprehensible on the basis of the practice of his community." In other words, what we have represented in the exception is the life-style of the late-first-century church that Matthew knew.

John P. Meier advances an interpretation that seems plausible—and closes the loophole. He says that the Greek word translated into our English versions as "unchastity" refers here to "incestuous union." Then the so-called exception applies to

unlawful marriages. Meier says that the church
put into Jesus' prohibition of divorce the clarifica-
tion that this was not to be used to countenance an
incestuous marriage contracted before a believer's
baptism. If Meier is correct, then for Christian
partners who marry in good faith and according to
the law, there is no possibility of divorce. Marriage
is for life, "till death us do part."

Who is correct? And does it matter? To fall to
quarreling over the statement about unchastity is
ourselves to fall into the trap the Pharisees built
for Jesus! To insist on any particular interpretation of that statement is to erect a legalism that
is as fruitless as the legalism Jesus wanted to go
beyond. Whether or not Jesus allowed for an exception to his proscription of divorce—and
whether or not that exception applies to sexual
infidelity or only to incestuous marriages—the
clear teaching of Matthew 19:3–9 must not be ob-
scured: The intent of God in Creation was that
male and female be joined in a permanent union.
Upon that intent is grounded Jesus' call to fidelity.
To divert attention from this call is itself an act of
infidelity to scripture.

To interpret this passage from Matthew as a call
to lifelong faithfulness will seem to some a hard
teaching. Isn't marriage difficult enough? Why
add to it the requirement of sworn faithfulness
"till death us do part"? Is not this a counsel of
perfection? Did not Jesus himself raise the stakes
to an impossible sum by interpreting the Seventh
Commandment to read, "But I say to you that
every one who looks at a woman lustfully has already committed adultery with her in his heart"

(Matt. 5:28)? Who can remain truly faithful to his or her spouse if even lustful thoughts are judged unfaithful? Isn't it as unrealistic to expect men and women to shun divorce and remarriage as it is unrealistic to expect that they can avoid lustful thoughts? If those be the rules of the game, who will not be found a loser?

Consider, however, the difficulty of the married state without Christ's call to fidelity. If there be no such call, what do we have? Then marriage is either some kind of bondage, in which one sex is regarded as created for the pleasure of the other, or it is a state of anarchy, in which there is no true bonding. Which of those is worse is hard to say; neither sexual bondage nor sexual anarchy is very appealing.

Perhaps our most perceptive novelist of domestic affairs is John Updike. When one reads such novels as *Couples, Marry Me,* and the trilogy of Rabbit Angstrom stories, one has the feeling that all American marriages are doomed to failure—or at least to some kind of uneasy peace. A comment comes to mind that is attributed to W. H. Auden on a visit to America: "I never saw so many happy people and so many unhappy marriages." If we are to take Updike's view of marriage as accurate, the missing ingredient is fidelity. His people hop in and out of the beds of others' wives and husbands as easily as they dive into one another's swimming pools.

It is when we read the Creation narratives in Genesis with the insight given us by Jesus that we understand that God made us male and female for something other than mere coupling: God made us for oneness, for bonding. To seek union with the other in obedience to Christ's call to loyalty—that is the heart of the Christian understanding of marriage.

Neither Law nor Love

We need to return to a statement made in the opening paragraph of this chapter, that loyalty—not law or romantic love—is what holds marriages together. It is when marriage based on fidelity is seen as an alternative to marriage based on love or law that its peculiar and particular nature is understood.

Fidelity—obedience to Christ's call—needs to be understood by comparison and contrast with two other models of marriage available to us. And these are models for which there is biblical warrant. One is the notion of marriage as based on romantic love; the other is the notion of marriage as based on law. Let us look at each.

The idea that marriages could be held together by law was the state of affairs that was represented to Jesus by the Pharisees who questioned him. They came to him from the tradition of the Torah. Marriage was regulated by God's commandments. What held marriage together was obedience to the rules God had established. And included in those laws was a rule permitting divorce under certain circumstances. The logic of such a relationship is clear: Marriage is based on rules. If one partner does not obey the rules, the relationship may be sundered. If a woman is guilty of "indecency" (Deut. 24:1), her husband has a legal (and therefore moral) right to give her a bill of divorce and put her out of the house. Of course the rules stipulate that she has rights; she must be given a bill of divorce, so she is free to marry again. She cannot be tossed aside like an outworn or torn garment; she must be returned to the marriage marketplace with some salability.

The attempt to regulate marriage by rules proves self-defeating. The very argument that was brought to Jesus proves that. The followers of one rabbi wanted to limit the grounds of divorce to unchastity and adultery. Another school wanted the grounds to be nearly anything the husband found distasteful. In such circumstances, what protection has the particular marriage? The institution is protected against easy abuse, but individual husbands can do awful things to individual wives. Where there is a law there is always a loophole.

In our culture the legal bond that once held marriages together has largely been replaced by the emotional one. Romantic love is seen as the glue that bonds the partners in marriage. A man and woman meet, fall in love, and, as long as love lasts, stay married. But let one partner cease to love the other or find a third person to love, and the marriage comes unstuck. The courts will not require that one partner prove that the other is guilty of any sexual infidelity. Incompatibility— the triumph of hate over love—is sufficient grounds for divorce.

The Bible does not ignore sexual love between husband and wife. An entire book of the Bible, the Song of Solomon, is a celebration of sexual attraction. Among the narratives of our forebears in the faith are love stories. Isaac fell in love with Rebekah at first sight; Jacob worked fourteen years to win the hand of Rachel; David fell in love with Bathsheba and, although theirs was an illicit romance, the result was marriage and the birth of Solomon, one of Israel's greatest kings. There is an old saw, "Where there is marriage without love, there will be love without marriage." The Bible does not fly in the face of that truth.

Nevertheless it is not to the tradition honoring romantic love or to the legal tradition represented in Deuteronomy 24:1 that Jesus appeals. His appeal is to the intention of the Creator in making humans male and female: that the two should become one. Fidelity to that intention, expressed as loyalty to the marriage partner, is the model for Christians in marriage.

Love and law are not wholly excluded from the regulation of the married life. The biblical notion of fidelity is best understood as resolve (a word that includes the letters L-O-V-E). It is love plus resolution. It is what is called in the Old Testament "steadfast" love. The model is given in the book of Hosea, which is best read as a parable. God is the offended spouse, Israel the offending one. At first God is angry, vows revenge, will break off the relationship. But finally God repents of that intent and says:

> My heart recoils within me,
>   my compassion grows warm and tender.
> I will not execute my fierce anger . . . ;
> for I am God and not man,
>   the Holy One in your midst,
>   and I will not come to destroy.
>   —Hosea 11:8b–9

The difference between resolve and romantic love is illustrated by the views of two contemporaries. The perils of romantic love were described by a once-divorced man, writing in the *New York Times Magazine.* He described his relationship with a woman with whom he had fallen in love. As long as the relationship remained an affair he was perfectly happy. But as soon as it took on the aura of permanence, it turned sour. He said that he could get along with her very well if they didn't live together as man and wife.

A woman in her sixties, who wrote a piece for the daily *New York Times,* described what she had learned from three marriages—the third and final one being a happy bonding. She spoke of this bond to her husband as including what she called "the most basic commitment of all, that one of us, in Emily Dickinson's words, will 'shut the other's gaze down.' " That is what the Bible understands as fidelity.

The plight of the man who could not stand a relationship that seemed permanent is perhaps a caricature of modern attitudes. But it has an all-too-familiar ring. Where love alone is conceived as the true bond between man and woman, loyalty takes a back seat. Or, to shift the metaphor, it is eased out the back door. Whereas in the biblical notion, love that is not a component of resolve is not love at all.

Grounding a Christian sexual ethic on the call of Christ to lifelong fidelity is not a quick and easy solution to the sexual crisis of our generation. A call to fidelity is no easier to hear and to answer than the call to love one's enemies, or take up one's cross, or part with one's worldly goods. But it is a constant in a culture of changing values and rules and customs. It is a fixed star by which every married couple may steer. It is rooted and grounded not only in the call of Christ but in the very purpose of the Creator. Husbands and wives may try to manage their marriages by love or laws; neither will prove infallible. But the call of Christ to fidelity summons husbands and wives to go beyond love or legality. It is a daily challenge; it makes marriage a lifelong career. And because fidelity is grounded in the intention of the Creator, it carries with it a guarantee, an assurance that, despite ups and downs, the marriage will be fruitful.

9

The Call
to Dispossession

And behold, one came up to him, saying, "Teacher, what good deed must I do, to have eternal life?" And he said to him, "Why do you ask me about what is good? One there is who is good. If you would enter life, keep the commandments." He said to him, "Which?" And Jesus said, "You shall not kill, You shall not commit adultery, You shall not steal, You shall not bear false witness, Honor your father and mother, and, You shall love your neighbor as yourself." The young man said to him, "All these I have observed; what do I still lack?" Jesus said to him, "If you would be perfect, go, sell what you possess and give to the poor, and you will have treasure in heaven; and come, follow me." When the young man heard this he went away sorrowful; for he had great possessions.
—Matthew 19:16–22

Jesus holds a first mortgage on all that you and I possess. We own it and we have the use of it, just as we possess and inhabit houses on which the bank or savings and loan holds a first mortgage. But at any moment Jesus may call us to dispose of our possessions in order to benefit some person or

cause that needs our support. Just as the bank
may choose to foreclose, so Jesus has a claim on all
we possess. To be called to be a disciple of Jesus is
to acknowledge this claim on our money, houses,
barns, lands, silver, clothes, cars, stocks, jewels,
antiques, and collectibles. Such is the teaching of
Jesus' encounter with the rich young man. Let us
examine the story in some detail.

The meeting comes about because the man has
evidently heard that Jesus teaches a new way of
life. The man reminds us of people in our society;
he has discovered that having a lot of money does-
n't necessarily mean that one feels fulfilled and
right with God. Either that or he is testing Jesus'
new movement, to see what kind of demands it
makes. A well-placed Jew, certainly he knows the
teachings of the Pharisees (keep the Law), of the
Essenes (be an ascetic and wait for the Coming), of
the Saduccees (follow the tradition), and of the
Zealots (join the revolution against Rome). Like
modern folk with more money than joy, he has a
cafeteria of ideologies from which to choose. And
so he comes to this new teacher to see what life-
style or piety Jesus is offering. Whether the man
is a serious seeker of truth and righteousness or
merely a dilettante, we do not know or care. Something moves him to be open to what Jesus might
say. And so he asks, "What good deed must I do,
to have eternal life?" He assumes the life pleasing
to God and likely to be rewarded by God depends
upon one's behavior.

We can imagine a modern seeker going to a
noted philosopher, or Zen Master, or Indian guru,
or the writer of a popular book on psychology and
asking a similar question. It is not a frivolous in-

quiry. Would not any of us gladly change places with that man and have the chance to ask Jesus, once and for all, What good deed must I do, to have eternal life? Shall I go as a foreign missionary? Shall I sell all that I possess? Shall I take a vow of chastity? Shall I commit myself to full-time Christian service? Shall I vow never to drink, smoke, commit fornication, swear, or steal? Shall I promise to speak the gospel to anyone and everyone that I meet? Shall I go and be with the poor?

These are but some of the answers that contemporary religious leaders offer to those who want to know the good deed that is essential to eternal life. In *Teaching a Stone to Talk,* Annie Dillard tells of meeting for the first time a neighbor boy of nine and his young mother. Each is on pins and needles until Annie is asked, Have you accepted the Lord Jesus as your personal Savior? The mother tells Annie that she has joined Rev. Jerry Falwell's congregation, and Annie knows that the young woman has made a commitment to ask everyone she meets if that person has been saved. That is the one good deed she must do.

The young man in Matthew's narrative asks Jesus about his good deed; he would settle at one stroke all doubts about being in or out of God's favor. He is in good company. As a young monk Martin Luther wrestled with this question year after year until he finally wrung from scripture his answer: Put your whole trust in Jesus Christ as your Savior and you will have eternal life. John Wesley searched for years until, sitting in a Moravian meeting, he had his heart "strangely warmed." The history of the Western world has been greatly affected by young people who have asked and asked, "What good deed must I do to inherit eternal life?" and have lived out the answer they found.

Jesus' response is not what we expect. Instead of giving a pious or even profound answer, he seems to brush aside the question. He says, "Why do you ask me about what is good? One there is who is good. If you would enter life, keep the commandments." It is an old trick of religious leaders to frame the answer to serious questions in such a way that the burden is immediately put back on the asker. A cardinal rule of spiritual teachers seems to be: Don't let the seeker put you on the spot; put the monkey on *his* back.

The young man doesn't want the monkey on his back. He tries to pass the responsibility back to Jesus, asking, "Which [commandment]?" There were some six hundred commandments that the pious Jew felt obliged to obey. The young man wants Jesus to pick out the few he thinks are special. We may suppose that Jesus is greatly tempted to lay on the young man his summary of the commandments: "You shall love the Lord your God with all your heart, and with all your soul, and with all your mind, and with all your strength. . . . You shall love your neighbor as yourself" (Mark 12:30–31). What great religious leader is not ready with his special agenda?

However, Jesus is not playing that game; he puts the monkey back on the young man. He reviews the commandments of God as they are given in the Decalogue: "You shall not kill, You shall not commit adultery, You shall not steal, You shall not bear false witness, Honor your father and mother." Then Jesus adds the summary statement, "You shall love your neighbor as yourself."

There, it's all laid down. The young man has been told *what he already knows!* It is said that you cannot teach anyone what they do not know already; and Jesus, being a good teacher, has reached back into the tradition that he shares with the young man and pointed out what both of them know: If you would be like a tree planted by rivers of water, learn to know, love, and obey the Law of God.

This doesn't satisfy the young man. He lets Jesus know that he is dead serious; he is not playing some kind of religious game. He counters with, "All these I have observed; what do I still lack?" He has a spiritual hunger that goes beyond the ordinary. He has kept the commandments; he has not committed adultery, has not killed or stolen, has honored his parents, and has tried, to the best of his ability, to deal fairly and justly with his neighbor. And yet all this has not brought him peace of mind. Like the young Luther, who gave up studying law to become a monk in hopes of finding God's favor, this young man has tried his best to please God. His question, "What do I still lack?" is haunting.

Now he and Jesus are no longer talking—if they ever were—about philosophy or theology or ethics. They are talking about this man's existence. Each has, in a sense, played out his language game; now the games are over. The man's life is on the line. He is asking Jesus, in effect, If you are sent from God, share with me the life you have with God; tell me your secret.

Jesus lays it right out: "If you would be perfect,

go, sell what you possess and give to the poor, and
you will have treasure in heaven; and come, follow
me." Jesus might have said, "Follow me, and I will
make you [a fisher] of men." Or "Take up [your]
cross and follow me." Or, "Go . . . and make disciples of all nations." We have heard these put for-
ward, in Jesus' own name, as that which we must
do if we truly would receive the gift of eternal life.
But Jesus says none of those things. He says, "If
you would be perfect, go, sell what you possess and
give to the poor, and you will have treasure in
heaven; and come, follow me."

Key Words

What are the key words in Jesus' invitation? "If
you would be perfect"? "Go, sell what you possess"? "Give to the poor"? "Come, follow me"? A
model of Christian discipleship could be fashioned
from each of those phrases. In truth, that has already happened.

There are members of Holiness sects that would
very likely seize on Jesus' invitation to perfection
as the critical point in the encounter. They hold to
an ethic of Christian perfection, a belief in a second blessing of the Spirit, which leads the believer
beyond ordinary morality. I was once involved
with members of a Holiness congregation from
Los Angeles in a cooperative youth work project.
On a Maundy Thursday we agreed that the kids
should have an outing. The lay leaders of the Holiness group ruled out anything as secular as a pic-
nic. We took the kids to visit Forest Lawn
Cemetery!

Others would see the key words in Jesus' invitation to be "Go, sell what you possess." They believe it is crucial to get rid of the encumbrance of worldly possessions. There is the story that Francis of Assisi, having decided to follow Christ, met a beggar and stripped off his fine clothes and gave them away.

Some would emphasize the giving of money to the poor, as though solidarity with the poor were the key to eternal life. In his 1987 TV series, *God and Politics,* Bill Moyers interviewed a Methodist minister from the United States who had sold everything and gone to live with the poor in Nicaragua. In his conversation with Bill, the man quoted from the Gospel story of Jesus and the rich young man as a rationale for his actions.

Still others would say that selling and giving away were means to the true deed that procures eternal life, which is following after Jesus. Thomas à Kempis wrote a devotional classic called *The Imitation of Christ.* That one may literally go and do what Christ did is a notion that will not die.

Which of these phrases is the keystone of Jesus' invitation? None, and yet all. If we take the whole narrative seriously, as we have tried to do, then no single phrase is more important than any other, anymore than one of the commandments is more important than another. The entire invitation to the young man is important, every part. The sum of the parts is what matters.

Are we to believe, then, that Jesus makes the same invitation to each of us? If we would be perfect—as our Father in heaven is perfect—must we sell all, give the money to the poor, and follow Jesus? Each of our commentators would answer those questions in a slightly different way.

John Meier writes (p. 220): "[Matthew], with his OT background, understands [perfect] in terms of whole-hearted, complete dedication to God. . . . 'If you wish to be perfect' is parallel to 'if you wish to enter life' . . . and means the same thing. . . . On this 'perfection,' this whole-hearted dedication to doing *justice* (5:20), to doing God's will completely, hangs every disciple's salvation."

Eduard Schweizer writes (p. 388): "Jesus did not demand of all people that they literally follow him, giving up home and possessions. . . . All one can say is that a special form of service is required of some and to them it is granted, giving them greater responsibility and a richer ministry."

Jack Dean Kingsbury writes (p. 92): "Matthew defines the greater righteousness [perfection] as doing the will of God. . . . But what is the hallmark . . .? Love: love toward God, and love toward the neighbor."

What then? Is the invitation for each and all of us, or just for some? If we do *not* believe that Jesus makes that invitation to each of us, then presumably he made it only to that young man and we are left to squeeze some precept out of the story as best we can. However, if we believe that it applies to each of us, are we then to read the story as an invitation to some kind of first-class sainthood, of which most of us are not capable? Or are we to suppose—believe—that the invitation is for all, if we but had the faith and trust to accept it? Or is it a challenge to see how many of us will put Jesus to the test and follow his command and see if indeed we have treasure in heaven?

Why should we not read this narrative in the same way as we have read the other narratives in this book? Why, as we read it, should we not listen for a call? To hear in it a call to dispossession is not to make it a rule that all Christians must sell everything and give the money to the poor. To hear in it a call is to accept the creative tension between what is and what might yet be, between the life we live as human beings in this world and the life to which Jesus summons us—without supposing that it is possible to resolve the tension in a single act or single moment.

The Call to Dispossession

If we would hear a call in this narrative, we must begin by identifying ourselves in the narrative with the rich young man. For it is our lot in life to be numbered among the "haves" of the world. If I have bread for two days and meet a man who has no bread for today, I am rich in comparison with him. He who has no bread for the day is poor indeed; and he who has bread and enough to tide him into the future is rich. We are all, at least some of the time, in the situation of the rich young man; we have more than we need, certainly more than others who are destitute and desperate. It is a generous and charitable act to give of what we have to the poor; God is pleased with that kind of generosity.

All the ethics of the Bible are on the side of sharing with the poor. We have no need to labor that point. And as Jesus himself reminded us, "The poor you have with you always," meaning that there are always persons in need of precious things that you do not need to sustain life. In any hour, on any day, there is always the possibility of taking what we do not need for the day's provision and giving it to someone who needs it more than we do. It is simply part of the human condition to be, at times, rich.

So when we talk about selling what we possess and giving to the poor, we are talking about a daily possibility—unless, of course, we take up the beggar's bowl like the holy men of India and live day by day from what others will give us. But even then, a holy man who has received a gift of rice will have next to him a holy man who has no rice for the day. Will he share? Will he give it away? He cannot, any more than we can, enter into a permanent state of poverty where he never is in the position of selling what he has and giving to the poor.

So to be one of the world's "haves" is not just a matter of being born into a First World country, into a capitalist society, into a booming economy that rewards everyone with more than his or her share of the world's goods. To a lesser or greater degree, to be rich is to be human; it means to be a creature that has more of life's necessities than another human creature. It means always to stand under the obligation to share with others.

That ought to get us past any Marxist reading of this text, in which the indictment of being rich applies only to the economic class that owns the means of production. That is not to make trivial the serious economic distinctions in this world. That would discredit the Magnificat of Mary, in which the young girl sings:

> He has shown strength with his arm,
> he has scattered the proud in the imagination of
>   their hearts,

he has put down the mighty from their thrones,
and exalted those of low degree;
he has filled the hungry with good things,
and the rich he has sent empty away.
                                    —Luke 1:51–53

God does indeed seem to have a bias toward the poor.

However, there does not seem to be any way— short of some act of unimaginable self-sacrifice— that we can commit poverty! We may elect a more simple life-style, like the Shakers of the last century or the Amish of our own. But there is a great difference between a more simple life-style and *poverty.* Besides, as David Hill gently reminds us (p. 283), in commenting on the story of Jesus and the rich young man, "Poverty is not a rule of universal application."

So we conclude that all our lives on earth we shall, for most of the time, be richer in possessions than others; all our lives we will be under the command of God to share with those less fortunate, with victims of our systems of distribution and production. One might try to imagine oneself an aboriginal in Australia, a member of a tribe in which all things are in common, so that none has more than the rest. But that is not something we can entertain as a serious possibility for ourselves.

It is our fate to be part of a system that divides human beings into "haves" and "have nots," the rich and the poor, those who have enough of this world's goods to live and be healthy and those who lack. There is no way we can change that.

What then is our call from Christ? How are we to live as rich Christians in a world that presents

us always with the poor? If we take this story of
the Rich Young Man as our paradigm, it yields
this: *We must be prepared at any moment to share
what we have, even to the last penny, with others
who are in need.* Jesus Christ has a first mortgage
on our possessions. If we are convinced that others
need our goods more than we do, we are called to
sacrifice them to that need. That does not mean
that they are not truly ours, for how can you share
what you do not possess? It seems clear from such
an example as Jesus' Parable of the Unjust Steward in Luke that the biblical steward managed the
affairs of his master as though the property were
indeed his own. In scripture human beings are the
stewards of God's creation. The call of Jesus to "sit
loose" to possessions does not mean that we are to
be careless or foolish or indiscriminate in giving
things away. Just as Christian marriage is a lifelong adventure of discovery, just as family life in
Christ is a lifelong adventure in relationships, so
is the ownership of goods a lifelong adventure in
management.

And if there is an ungodly sorrow in our lives,
might it not be that we are holding too tightly to
our possessions? If our lives seem too small, too
cramped, too narrow, is it possible that we have
measured them by the amount of this world's
goods and money and artifacts that we possess?
We have myths in our culture of the unhappy
miser, whose hoarded gold brings him or her only
misery. But might it not be that many of us are
miserable directly in proportion to our reluctance
to give when we are asked, to share when we find
others in need, to hoard, to save against too many
rainy days?

Jesus had a great deal to say about money. And in his teachings there is little about the evils of belonging to the class of the rich at the expense of the poor. But there is a lot about the sadness and destruction that fall upon those who trust in riches, who make being rich an end in itself, who hold on to their riches like grim death. Note the Parable of the Rich Man and Lazarus, the Parable of the Rich Fool, the teaching that it is easier for a camel to go through the eye of a needle than for a rich man to enter the kingdom of heaven.

Contrast our story of the Rich Young Man with that of Zacchaeus, the tax collector. Under the spell of Jesus' friendship, Zacchaeus volunteered to give away much of his wealth. Contrast the sorrow of the Rich Young Man with the joy of the man in Jesus' Parable of the Treasure in the Field, who goes away and for joy sells all that he has to buy the field with the treasure in it—assuming that the treasure is the kingdom of heaven, for which one joyfully gives up or gives away all that one has.

Mind you, this is not a chapter about giving generously to the church! It is about a call to a life-style in which one holds on to one's possessions with hands ready at any moment to open and give generously to alleviate the suffering of the poor. In conceivable situations, that might involve *selling everything*. Why not? What does it profit a man if he gain the whole world and forfeits his life?

I know a man, similar to me in age and station, who went to live in a community of caring; he handed over his assets to the group and accepted a much more simple life-style. The motto of that

group is "Live simply, that others may simply
live." Whether or not we all are called to join such
a community is not the issue. But that is near to
what this passage and story are about!

During the 1960s a number of young persons in
the United States tried their hand at living in
communes, where—like the early Christian
church—"They had all things in common." Like
other utopian communes in America—the Shakers, Oneida, Brook Farm—they didn't last. But in
an affluent society one has got to be tempted, at
least once, to see what it is like to be out from
under the weight of so many possessions.

In C. P. Snow's novel *Time of Hope,* a man
named Martineau, owner of a firm of lawyers,
gives his practice to his partner and takes to the
road as a poor itinerant preacher. Martineau's
friends are baffled and one of the principal characters in the novel is greatly inconvenienced, since
Martineau was his patron. Martineau is regarded
by everyone, including the author of the novel, as
being slightly dotty. Snow's heroes are scientists,
who help develop radar and the atom bomb, university professors, lawyers, doctors, civil servants—people who are actively engaged in trying
to make society either better or less harsh. It
seems impossible for contemporary people to
imagine anyone finding true fulfillment in a life of
abnegation. Ours is not a self-denying age. If someone wants to sell everything and give to the poor,
we are more likely to turn for an explanation to
Freud of Vienna or to Jung of Zurich than to Jesus
of Nazareth.

Nevertheless, the import of the narrative of the
Rich Young Man seems clear enough: Jesus calls

those who would follow him to be prepared to dispose of their worldly goods and possessions if they become a hindrance to discipleship.

Whether or not to dispossess oneself would seem to be an individual decision: There is no implication that all Christians ought to opt for an ascetic life-style. But nevertheless, Jesus holds a first mortgage on all that we who would follow him possess. And we who are the third or fourth or fifth generation of people who sold everything in Russia or Germany or Northern Ireland or China or Korea to come to America to find a better life, should we find it impossible to understand how anyone would sell everything for a second chance, a new beginning? Not that a second chance is always a fat chance. In the nineteenth-century first-person accounts in *Pioneer Women,* by Joanna Stratton, are some harrowing tales of what it was like for well-brought-up women from New York and Pennsylvania and Ohio to give up everything and move to the Kansas frontier. Some were driven mad by filth, loneliness, the wind, isolation. Nevertheless, our tribal memory cherishes those forebears who sold all that they possessed in hopes of a better future. Voluntary dispossession may be an adventure, a lightening oneself for a trip into the unknown. It often seems in our society that there are few true adventures left. This may be one that some of us might yet be called upon to try.

10

The Call to Servant Leadership

Then the mother of the sons of Zebedee came up to him, with her sons, and kneeling before him, she asked him for something. And he said to her, "What do you want?" She said to him, "Command that these two sons of mine may sit, one at your right hand and one at your left, in your kingdom." But Jesus answered, "You do not know what you are asking. Are you able to drink the cup that I am to drink?" They said to him, "We are able." He said to them, "You will drink my cup, but to sit at my right hand and at my left is not mine to grant, but it is for those for whom it has been prepared by my Father." And when the ten heard it, they were indignant at the two brothers. But Jesus called them to him and said, "You know that the rulers of the Gentiles lord it over them, and their great men exercise authority over them. It shall not be so among you; but whoever would be great among you must be your servant, and whoever would be first among you must be your slave; even as the Son of man came not to be served but to serve, and to give his life as a ransom for many."

—*Matthew 20:20–28*

The human spirit has a built-in push to greatness. Like corks held under water, persons have an impulse to bob to the top. Like the young hero of Horatio Alger's story, we are bound to rise. In a *New York Times Magazine* article about an ambitious second-generation Taiwanese boy, this impulse was entitled "The Drive to Excel." But that drive is not limited to immigrants; it is universal. There is ample reminder of this in the narrative in chapter 20 of Matthew, in which the mother of James and John comes to Jesus to ask that her boys get top jobs.

She is not just another pushy parent, this woman who begs, "Command that these two sons of mine may sit, one at your right hand and one at your left, in your kingdom." She is Everymother. Or, if you prefer, Everyparent. Which parents do not dream of their children achieving greatness? Getting the best jobs? Rising to the top of the heap? Sitting with the powerful and the respected?

With some parents, surely, thwarted personal ambition is projected onto a son or daughter. Why else would a woman scrub floors so that her daughter could go to college? Or a father take on a second job so that his son might go to medical school? Why else do parents, when they gather after hours, spend so much time talking about their hopes for their children? These hopes are often voiced as narratives about success on the Little League field or in the sixth-grade spelling bee. But the bottom line is always: I hope my kid becomes someone special!

It is parochial to suppose that ambition is limited to parents of the middle class, in suburbia, and in the United States. Our biblical passage suggests that such ambition is universal. Here is a fisherman's wife of the first century, in an obscure corner of the Roman Empire, grasping at the possibility that her two sons—without education, breeding, or financial backing—might sit as princes in Messiah's kingdom.

In Matthew's narrative, Zebedee's wife is not the only illustration of the push to greatness. What of Jesus himself? Look at him! He has the mother kneeling at his feet, begging favors, like a poor widow asking for patronage from a ward boss. Like an impoverished noblewoman groveling before Louis XIV. Like a thief begging a Manchu emperor for pardon. This is the image of greatness that recurs in countless fairy tales, histories, case studies, and newspaper accounts: One person has such power to grant favors that others come and kowtow.

We have been taught to despise that kind of scene. Our democratic spirits cry out against it. We want Jesus to tell the woman to rise to her feet, to stop that degrading exercise. But he calmly asks her what it is she wants! He does not deny his kingship—nor that his kingship merits the kind of reverence the woman offers him. We may wish he would take her by the hand, draw her to her feet, and ask her to discuss things as equals. But no; he says, "What do you want?" He accepts the role of oriental potentate, who has the duty to listen to his subjects and to grant requests, if they be reasonable and within his power.

What the woman asks for is audacious; she wants top jobs for her two boys. She wants James to sit on one side of the throne and John on the other. Presumably the persons who sat at the right and left hand of an oriental monarch shared in his power. When they addressed the public, they spoke for him; if he leaned to right or left and asked advice, it was within their power—by whispering in his ear—to give and take life, seize property, pardon capital offenses.

Who of us has not dreamed of such power? Why else do people wager millions on lotteries, if not to be rich and therefore powerful and able to satisfy any whim, to command the service and loyalty of others? Of what use is money if in some sense it does not—so to speak—put you at the king's right hand, where wishes can quickly be translated into deeds?

In our biblical narrative, the other ten disciples are indignant when they hear what is asked for the two brothers. And why not? There must have been rivalry among the Twelve. Who of them had not dreamed of being Jesus' right- or left-hand man? Why else would they be indignant at the power grab of the brothers? Where is there a closely knit group of workers in which there is not elbowing for the top jobs and the best seats? When in the whole history of the world have there been a dozen men, tied tightly in an enterprise, who were not concerned about rank?

If we have any doubt that human beings yearn to rule over others, Jesus dispels it with his reference to "the Gentiles" (meaning almost everybody in the world). "You know that the rulers of the Gentiles lord it over them, and their great men exercise authority over them" (Matt. 20:25). He reminds the disciples of what they already know: The push for the top jobs is what men and women of this world are mightily inclined toward. We do not need any more reminding that indeed there is built into human nature a push to greatness.

Our world, as mirrored in this narrative from Matthew, is one in which there is a constant shove toward the top of the heap. Sometimes it is the push of individuals for their own greatness and glory; sometimes it is the push of parents for the top jobs for their children. But that is how it is, folks, in the real world. It is our destiny to live in a world where there is fierce and constant competition for the best seats. That was true long before Charles Darwin described the survival of the fittest. It is as true of communist societies as of capitalist ones. It is as true of women as of men. One might prefer to live in a world where cooperation replaced competition, but we cannot invent the kind of world we would like to live in. We live in the world as it is.

This is not indisputable: Some folks insist we can have a world that is ruled by cooperation, from which competition for the top jobs and the best seats is eliminated. They promote noncompetitive games; they form co-ops; they make sharing the primary value in the nursery class. Some call our attention to the classroom behavior of Native American children, who are reluctant to recite if they show up their peers. But that is merely a bias against individualism; certainly the various Native American tribes were competitive enough when it came to protecting game lands from other tribes. And what fun are games in which you are not allowed to win? And don't co-ops end up in competition with one another? If it isn't always a dog-eat-dog world, certainly it is a world in which people hanker mightily to be top dog.

The Call to Service

If indeed it is our destiny to live in a world of competition, what is our call? It is a summons from Jesus to live in the Christian community as the servants of one another. "The essence of discipleship consists not in the enjoyment of privilege but in rendering service to others" (Kingsbury, p. 54). Jesus acknowledged that, among the Gentiles, it was common that the great should lord it over the rest and the rulers should exercise arbitrary authority. "It shall not be so among you," he said; "but whoever would be great among you must be your servant, and whoever would be first among you must be your slave." John Meier comments (p. 228), "Jesus first speaks of the servant, the person who freely puts himself at the disposition of others, and then radicalizes his statement with the image of the slave, the non-person who has no rights or existence of his own, who exists solely for others."

This is what in the New Testament we previously named a Great Reversal. There are other Great Reversals, but none more startling. Those who aspire to be influential in the church are to seek not the top jobs or the chief seats but the interest and advancement of others. Elsewhere Jesus enunciated the Law of Reversal: "So the last will be first, and the first last" (Matt. 20:16). In this study we have seen the practical results of that reversal: We are to save our lives by losing them; we are to love our enemies; we are to forgive our debtors. And now we have one more instance of it: We are to seek greatness by being servants.

Several of our commentators agree that it is in the church that this servant role is to be exercised. "[This section] concludes the entire period in which the disciples are to learn what it means to live in the community of Jesus. Matthew 18 described how the community could live as a free congregation of brothers without having any members placed in positions of superiority and control, held together only by brotherly service, imposed upon all" (Schweizer, p. 398). "This world cannot supply the model for leadership in the church. Church leadership is modeled on the paradox of the cross, the inversion of all values and ambitions. . . . Church leaders who derive their tools and signs of power from this world betray the gospel of Jesus" (Meier, pp. 228–229).

A word of caution: The call is to servanthood, not to servility. A common misunderstanding of Jesus' teachings is that Christians are to be servile—never to aspire to greatness, always to think poorly of themselves. That is a common but complete misunderstanding of what Jesus asked of us. Jesus did not say, Whoever among you would be great, let them be servile. That would have been relatively easy for us to manage. Many of us are experts at playing Poor Little Me, who can't do anything good or right—certainly not anything noteworthy. Jesus didn't ask for that. He asked for something much more difficult: that we put the interests of others ahead of ourselves.

We must be careful not to read into the term

"servant" purely sociological meaning. We think of Rose and Mr. Hudson in *Upstairs, Downstairs,* of Uncle Tom, of waiters, butlers, houseboys, Filipino gardeners—all the servant images of our society—and we suppose that is what Jesus calls us to be, a sort of religious Peace Corps, in which we run around looking for people to do good to, whether or not they want good done to them! Not so. What Jesus calls us to is the style and disposition of a servant, one whose chief concern is the interests of others. The servile person is concerned about himself or herself, to win the favor of others by being obsequious or humble; the servant is concerned about the health and welfare and well-being of others. If you would be great, Jesus told his disciples, aspire to serve your fellow disciples. If you and I aspire to greatness, we will find true greatness by seeking first to be the servants of others.

Jesus clearly put the emphasis on seeking the welfare of others rather than upon the lowly social status of the slave. For after saying, "Whoever would be great among you must be your servant," he added the reason for such a Great Reversal: "Even as the Son of man came not to be served but to serve, and to give his life as a ransom for many." It is the self-sacrificing of Christ on behalf of others that is our model, example, impetus, motivation for servanthood. This model constantly reminds us that a true servant is one who seeks the welfare of others, not one who despises social rank and prefers being a gardener to a corporate executive or who enjoys knuckling his forehead and saying Yes, sir! or Yes, ma'am! There is in our current society a reluctance on the part of some to

be part of a system in which a few are considered
of superior rank. So they opt out entirely from the
large institutions of society and go off and live in
classless societies of their own making. This is not
what Jesus intended. He intended what Paul
terms looking "not only to [your] own interests,
but also to the interests of others" (Phil. 2:4).

The Servant Image

There is a host of images in scripture that support this understanding of the true servant. Prominent among these is the cluster of images of the
Suffering Servant in Isaiah, chapters 40–55, in
which the Servant of God is pictured not as one
who is self-effacing but as one who brings justice
and righteousness to earth through suffering.

> He was despised and rejected by men;
> a man of sorrows, and acquainted with grief;
> and as one from whom men hide their faces
> he was despised, and we esteemed him not.
> —Isaiah 53:3

Such an image calls to mind such modern servants
of humanity as Gandhi, Martin Luther King, Jr.,
Sister Teresa, Kagawa, Dorothy Day, Jean
Vanier. The Servant in Isaiah is one who affects
the course of history, who is instrumental in
bringing God's will to pass in human affairs.

The servant image was never more clear than in
the hymn to Christ in Philippians, where it is said
of Jesus that he, "though he was in the form of
God, did not count equality with God a thing to be
grasped, but emptied himself, taking the form of

a servant" (Phil. 2:6–7). It is Jesus Christ in his incarnation and sacrificial death who is the final model and motivation for servanthood.

Servant Leadership

Robert K. Greenleaf spent most of his working life in management training for AT&T. In his book *Servant Leadership,* he describes what our society most needs. It is what Greenleaf calls the servant leader. This is a person who is chosen to guide a great institution—a corporation, a church, a university—because he or she has first displayed a capacity for and a disposition toward being a servant. Greenleaf does not find the concepts servant and leader at odds with one another. As a matter of fact, he insists that "the great leader is seen as servant first, and that simple fact is the key to his greatness." Greenleaf goes on to say that he sees a social movement developing in which only servant leaders will be followed. More and more, society mistrusts leaders whose chief interests are their own agendas and authority; more and more, people are looking for leaders whose first interest is the good of others.

That is an important point in Greenleaf's understanding of the servant leader. His service to others must past this difficult test: "Do those served grow as persons? Do they, *while being served,* become healthier, wiser, freer, more autonomous, more likely themselves to become servants?"

In the view of the author of Matthew, Jesus certainly would have passed such a test: "The Son of man came not to be served but to serve, and to give his life as a ransom for many." Jesus showed

his servant leadership in giving his life to set people free. The Gentiles of Jesus' day would have
scorned a book called *Servant Leadership;* for, as
Jesus told the disciples, "The rulers of the Gentiles lord it over them, and their great men exercise authority over them." In the Gentile world,
which knows not Christ, servant and leader are
contradictory terms. We who know the servant
Sovereign know differently.

One important thing remains to be said about
servant leadership. This is a kind of greatness no
one chooses. Rather, one is chosen for such service.
When the mother of James and John asks Jesus
for the right and left seats in his kingdom, he gives
two reasons why they cannot have them. First of
all, he questions whether or not they are able to
drink the cup that he will drink. The reference is
clearly to his impending suffering and death. The
route to the kind of greatness that the mother
wants for her sons leads through suffering and
death. Certainly she has not reckoned with that!
But also, Jesus says, the seats at his right and left
hand are not his to grant; they are for those for
whom they have been prepared by the Father in
heaven. Not only is greatness to be achieved by
being a servant; not only does it lead through suffering and death—ask Gandhi, King, Lincoln,
Raoul Wallenberg—but it is granted to those for
whom God has prepared it. Men and women are
chosen for greatness; they do not choose to be
great. They choose to be servants, following the
example of Christ; the Father in heaven chooses
them for greatness.

This is one of the insights of *Bearing the Cross,*
David Garrow's portrait of Martin Luther King,

Jr. The book shows a man upon whom the prophetic mantle fell against his wishes. King just happened to be on the scene in Montgomery, Alabama, when the bus boycott began—a young preacher newly come to town. He did not choose leadership; it sought him out and chose him. There is a saying in the civil rights movement: "If Rosa Parks had not sat down, Martin King would not have stood up." Events conspired to make King the leader of a movement. Robert Greenleaf, in describing the servant leader, has his order straight: One chooses to be a servant of the public; one is then chosen to be a leader.

Our call, then, is to servanthood: to have, as Paul puts it, "this mind among yourselves, which is yours in Christ Jesus" (Phil. 2:5); to seek the welfare of our brothers and sisters in Christ and of our neighbor; to be disposed to serve rather than to be served. If honor and respect come of all that or through all that, one is not to shun them or pretend to be surprised or play the no-account. But one does not choose that path in order to be great.

The world desperately needs servant leaders, those whom great institutions can trust to lead, because they are first and foremost committed to serving. None of us dare to aspire to be a Martin Luther, a Martin Luther King, Jr., an Abraham, an Abraham Lincoln, or a Joan of Arc. But we may—and must—aspire to be servants of one another, to seek the common rather than our own private good. This we can do; it is well within our capabilities. And if others should see our service and summon us to lead them—first within the church, then possibly in the university, in Congress, or in the corporation—we may trust the call of Christ and follow that path to greatness.

When I was growing up in a small town in western Pennsylvania, I saw the idea of the servant leader lived out. Charles Evans was an elder in our congregation and the superintendent of our Sunday school. He also happened to be the managing director of a steel mill, where I worked for two summers. He was a quiet, modest man who had been chosen during World War I to rescue an ailing company. When that summons came, he was on the faculty of a boys' school as an instructor in chemistry. But he left the classroom and took over the company and put it on its feet. He was by all odds the best loved and most respected worker in that plant.

I have been privileged to know several persons like Charles Evans—decent, dutiful, modest people, who carry heavy responsibilities with great cheerfulness and compassion. They made public service their first order of priority. They did not aspire to greatness. Greatness found them out. So will it find out any who allow the service of others to become their ruling passion.

11

*The Call
to Universal Mission*

*Now the eleven disciples went to Galilee, to the
mountain to which Jesus had directed them. And
when they saw him they worshiped him; but some
doubted. And Jesus came and said to them, "All
authority in heaven and on earth has been given to
me. Go therefore and make disciples of all nations,
baptizing them in the name of the Father and of
the Son and of the Holy Spirit, teaching them to
observe all that I have commanded you; and lo, I
am with you always, to the close of the age."*
                                    —Matthew 28:16–20

All disciples of Jesus Christ are called by him to
be involved in a universal mission. Both individual Christians and the various parts of Christ's
church stand under the Great Commission: "Go
therefore and make disciples of all nations, baptizing them in the name of the Father and of the Son
and of the Holy Spirit, teaching them to observe
all that I have commanded you." As Eduard
Schweizer correctly points out, the main verb in
that sentence, to which all else is subordinate, is
make. We who follow Jesus are commissioned to
summon men and women of all races and lands to

join us in his service. In order to accomplish that, we are to go, to baptize, and to teach. "It has taken [Matthew] a whole gospel to explain what being a disciple means . . . it means following Jesus by obeying his teaching, by accepting his fate of death and resurrection in one's own life, and by proclaiming him as Son of Man, Lord of the universe" (Meier, p. 370).

If Jesus is indeed what he claimed for himself, the One to whom all authority in heaven and on earth belongs, then all are to be brought into submission to his sovereignty. "By his death-resurrection, Jesus has received from the Father . . . total power over the *universe;* this is what enables him to initiate a *universal mission"* (Meier, p. 369). It is this universal sovereignty of Jesus, risen from the dead and glorified, that dominates the final scene of Matthew's Gospel. At his appearance some of the disciples fell on their knees in worship, while others were astounded and knew not what to do. But worshipers and doubters alike were charged: Make the sovereignty of Jesus effective over all creation. The earliest Christian confession was, Christ is Lord. The Great Commission is like unto it, Make Christ Lord. "The rule of Christ over the entire world is associated with universal discipleship" (Schweizer, p. 532).

That is not the reading of Matthew 28:16–20 that is familiar to most of us. We have been accustomed to a geographical rather than cosmological reading. It is the "go" in verse 19 that has been lifted up as the main verb in the sentence and as the central imperative in the commission. But while it is true enough that we are to "go into all the world" (Mark 16:15), going is just one dimension of the mandate. The aim or end is to "make disciples of all nations." The words that dominate the climactic scene in Matthew are cosmic rather than geographical: *"All* authority in heaven and on earth ... *all* nations ... *all* that I have commanded you" (emphasis added). Christ is the universal sovereign: All nations belong to him; all persons are his; all life is to be brought into subjection to him.

In the elect man, Jesus, not only all human beings but the whole creation has been elected to receive God's favor and fulfill God's will. And it is to be involved in this universal enterprise of God that we Christians are called.

A Drama in Three Acts

Christ summons us to complete the divine drama. For the Bible may be understood as a drama in three acts. In Act I, God sets out to restore the world to its original purpose. God calls Abraham and Sarah and promises to make them a numerous people and to establish them as a great nation, through whom all the peoples of the world will be blessed. At the end of Act I, the Hebrews are indeed numerous—but they are slaves in Egypt.

Act II sees the fulfillment of the promise to make of Abraham's descendants, now called Israel, a great nation. The climactic scene in Act II is the making of the covenant at Mount Sinai, with the giving of the Law through Moses. Having been liberated in the exodus, Israel is now estab-

lished as a nation with God's Law. And with the
Davidic kingship, Israel takes her place as one of
the notable nations of the world.

Act III sees the blessing of all nations through
Israel's Anointed One (Messiah). This blessing is
set in motion through the enthronement of Jesus
of Nazareth on the cross. Through his resurrection he is declared Savior and Sovereign. And in
Matthew 28:16–20 the risen and exalted Jesus appears, like Moses, on a mountain, and he sends his
Law (teaching) into all the world through the
agency of the eleven, who represent the tribes of
Israel.

In this divine drama all Christians are called to
participate; each has a part to play. Each, by vir-
tue of his or her baptism into Christ, is an actor.
None is excluded; all are included. It belongs to
the very nature of the Christian life to be part of
the universal mission. "Go therefore and make
disciples of all nations . . . teaching them to observe all that I have commanded you" applies just
as much to each of us as does Jesus' injunction to
"love your enemies" or "when you pray, go into
your room and shut the door."

The biblical witness is plain: From the call of
Abraham to the call of Saul of Tarsus, God was
choosing a special people as a divine mission to the
whole world. None was chosen for his or her sake
alone. The seeking, searching love of God is for all
humankind, not just for those who know God's
name, God's will, and God's purpose. The God of
the biblical drama is a God of intention as well as
love, a people is chosen to be God's own, both out
of love and with a divine purpose. The love and
purpose are not to be separated.

And what is true of God is true of the church: It is both the object of God's love and the agent of God's purpose. As has been truly said, mission is to the church as fire is to burning. Deny the church its universal mission, and you take from it what is essential to its nature. A church without mission is as unthinkable as God without purpose. The Great Commission is rooted in that purpose; that is its source and its legitimacy.

Say the word "mission," and to some it brings to mind the missionary going to convert the heathen and save souls. This implied imperialism grates on the sensibilities of many Christians. But there is a legitimate imperialism given the church that has little to do with universal truth or with who or who does not get into heaven. Christ said to the disciples, who represent the church, *"All* authority in heaven and on earth has been given to me. Go therefore and make disciples of *all* nations, . . . teaching them to observe *all* that I have commanded you" (emphasis added). The mandate is to go with every sense of having been fully commanded by God, allowing no place or persons to be excluded, and making plain the whole of Christ's teachings. The mission of the church is universal—worldwide, world-embracing, world-encompassing—whether or not we can prove that Christianity is universally true or superior to every other religion.

Given the history of wars of religion, it is vital that we resolutely deny to ourselves the notion that we engage in mission because we have the truth or that what we have is superior to what others know and believe. The energy of mission comes from obedience to Christ's call and from our

willingness to be the agents of God's purpose to
have mercy on all; it does not issue from our intention to do something good for God!

The difference between those two motivations is
enormous. Where the later view has prevailed—
the view that we have a superior truth to offer—
there have been wars of religion, enmities
between Christian and Jew, the denial in Christ's
name of human and civil rights, the burning of
heretics, and worse! But where the motivations
have been a devotion to Christ and a sharing of his
love for all kinds of persons, the story has been
quite different.

If despite our sorry history of bigotry and intol-
erance we are to hold to a worldwide missionary
calling of the church, we need to be clear always
about the context of that call. It comes to us in a
world that has seen a so-called "Christian nation," Germany, set out resolutely to destroy its
Jewish citizens. It comes to us in a world where
Protestants and Roman Catholics in Northern
Ireland are at each other's throats. It comes to us
in a world where religion marks the division
among peoples and defines them as enemies: Jew
from Muslim, Muslim from Christian, Hindu from
Muslim, Christian from Hindu. All too often religion has been used to justify the existence of
nation-states and to justify hostility between
nations.

But despite all of that, the call is to be involved
in universal mission. No people, no institutions,
no territories, no spheres of influence are to be
regarded as *not* standing under the authority that
Christ claimed for himself.

What Shall We Do?

Of course it is one thing to say that all disciples are to be involved in the universal mission. But what, in practical, concrete terms, are we to *do?* There are four ways in which Christians have traditionally been involved in universal mission. They represent a minimal obedience to Christ's call.

1. *We can tell the story.* Beginning with the activity of the eleven disciples, there has been a thin red line running throughout the history of the church. At times it has wavered, sometimes it has grown very faint, once in a while it has broadened like a great river, but it has never ceased. It is the continuing story of the missionary outreach of the church. And we have the responsibility to keep that story alive. The missionary journeys of Paul, recorded in the New Testament, form a first chapter. In what follows, each storyteller might call the roll in a different way. But it ought to include Augustine (England), Columba (Scotland), Carey and Scudder (India), Livingstone (Africa), Zwemer (Arabia), Marquette (America), Judson (Burma), Moffett and Underwood (Korea), Ricci (China), and Grenfell (Labrador). Each name calls to memory a story of courage, sacrifice, patience, devotion.

One should not suppose that the story ended in the nineteenth century; witness the remarkable events surrounding the captivity and release of missionary Ben Weir in 1984 and 1985. And the story is continually being told in fresh ways. In 1984, Yale historian Jonathan D. Spence published *The Memory Palace of Matteo Ricci,* an ac-

count of an early Jesuit missionary to China. Ricci
was an Italian who went to China in the late six-
teenth century in hopes of winning the cultured
elite to Christianity and of finally gaining an audience with the Chinese emperor.

We need to keep the story of missionary heroism
alive, just as the civil rights movement keeps alive
the story of Martin Luther King, Jr., and American democracy keeps alive the story of Lincoln's
birth in a log cabin. Our children and grandchildren deserve that much from us.

2. *We need to share the wealth.* There is a financial dimension to the universal mission of the
church. Through the heroism of our forebears,
there are churches on every continent and in
nearly every land. People in all nations have been
baptized, and the church is teaching them the
commandments of Christ. But churches are volun-
teer organizations, requiring financial support.
Paul took up collections in his congregations for
the relief of the church in Jerusalem. And it remains one of the requirements that those who
have more than they need share with Christians
and churches who have less. It is within the reach
of all of us to answer the call to mission with
financial support. It may be the least we can do,
but at least we can do that much!

Some years ago churchwomen established the
Fellowship of the Least Coin. Women all over the
world took an offering for mission and ministry;
they each brought to their church the smallest
coin in their currency. It was a powerful demonstration that everyone can do something, and
when everyone's contribution was brought together it added up to a considerable sum.

3. *We can work to heal the divisions in the church.* A universal mission has as its corollary a church universal, what some call the church catholic. Surely it is part of our call to do what is within our power and our reach to heal the divisions in the church. There cannot be one Sovereign and several churches. There can only be one church, one people of God. And whatever we can do to make that a reality, we are called to do.

We did not invent denominations; we only inhabit them. But we can avoid the sin of denominationalism, which is surely as heinous as the sin of racism or anti-Semitism. We didn't invent race or culture; we are born Anglo-Saxon, African, Asian, Native American, Hispanic. But we decry racism—race raised to an absolute, a rule of exclusion, a theory of superiority. So it is with denominations; we were born Presbyterians, Baptists, Anglicans. But we do not need to make those divisions absolute, to exclude others, to assert superiority, to be imperialistic. Rather, as we seek to diminish racism, we can work to diminish denominationalism.

4. *We can make friends across national boundaries.* That may sound simplistic and unheroic. But it is something that a great many Christian people have done with surprising results. All of us have the capacity for friendship. And to many of us the opportunity is given to establish friendships across national lines. Communities have students from other countries going to schools and colleges. Many high schools are involved in student exchange programs. Americans travel abroad in increasing numbers; the number of tourists coming to America from other nations increases yearly.

Most of us have opportunities to make at least one
friend from another country.

Salt and Light

These ways of being involved in universal mission are not particularly dramatic. On the face of
it, they do not sound terribly effective. Not if one
conceives of universal mission in metaphors
drawn from military conquest, colonization, and
business. But the history of missions ought to
warn us away from military, colonial, and commercial metaphors. Such metaphors are not to be
trusted.

Military metaphors, enshrined in hymns such
as "Onward, Christian Soldiers," imply that the
nations are to be subdued, conquered, defeated.
But Christ did not command the eleven to go forth
to conquer the world, but to baptize and teach.

The colonial metaphor, with its suggestion of
occupation, plantations, and the eventual trans-
formation of other cultures, also needs to be given
up. In the southwestern United States in the cen-
turies after the Spanish came, it was the practice
of the church to send European priests to the Indian pueblos. The priests often acted like colonial
governors. In *Death Comes for the Archbishop,*
Willa Cather gives an unforgettable portrait of
this colonial style of mission work. But Jesus did
not say, Go and colonize in my name. He said, "Go
and make disciples . . . baptize . . . teach what I
have commanded you."

We also need to surrender the commercial metaphor, as though all the people in the world con-
stituted a vast religious market, potential

consumers of Christianity waiting for the right salesmen and saleswomen to arrive and convince them to buy the product. In the marketing metaphor, churches and church outposts then become like branch stores or branch banks, where everything gets quantified. And the successful mission is one that can point with pride to its many outlets and its host of customers. But Jesus did not say, Go into the world and sell Christianity to all nations. He said, "Go and make disciples . . . baptize . . . teach."

We shouldn't be surprised at the ease with which we have adopted the military, the colonial, and the commercial metaphors for conceiving of the universal mission. Jesus did say, after all, "Make disciples of all *nations*" (emphasis added). As members of a nation-state we are accustomed to think of dealing with citizens of other nation-states in military, colonial, and commercial metaphors. It is a natural way of thinking. But it is not the biblical way of thinking of mission. So we are led to look for other metaphors.

Jesus gave us two figures of speech for mission, each of which is more compatible with telling the story, sharing the wealth, healing divisions, and making friends. He said to his disciples, "You are the salt of the earth. . . . You are the light of the world" (Matt. 5:13–14). His disciples are to be a visible presence in the world, which in some way seasons and preserves that world. Salt and light are not military, not colonial, not commercial metaphors. Nor are they very romantic or heroic. But they arise out of Christ's command.

The metaphors of salt and light suggest that one can obey the Great Commission in quite ordinary,

everyday ways. Both salt and light are domestic
images: a pinch of salt to season and flavor food,
a candle put on a stand. They imply a vital, essential role for the home-loving, everyday, garden-
variety Christian. Not everyone is to go as a
missionary to China; not every Christian has the
skills or stamina to salvage the human wrecks in
our major cities. But each of us can be salt and
light. That is what we are when we tell the story,
share the wealth, heal the divisions, and make
friends.

Salt and light apply both to the church scattered and the church gathered. The congregation
gathered for worship in its building on Fourth and
Main is a light to the world; its members working
in schools, homes, shops, hospitals, and offices are
the church scattered in the world like salt. All we
need to do is be willing to make a difference wherever we are in this needy world.

A word of caution: The phrase "needy world" is
apt to lead us away from the essential meanings
of salt and light. If you ask the world what it
wants, it will not reply, Give us salt, give us light.
John says in the prologue to his Gospel that when
the Light of the World came, the world hated him,
because its deeds were evil. The world does not
think it needs light to dispel its darkness, nor does
it think it needs salt to season and save it from rot.
The world thinks it needs money, power, comfort,
therapy, law and order, pleasure, beauty. To be
salt and light in the world may, at times, be as
difficult as taking a sailing ship to China or
preaching to headhunters or living in a rain forest.

In sum, we may not find much honor in being

salt in the office or light in the community. People will resist the teachings of Christ, whether we speak them aloud or silently act them out. People will resist the implication of Baptism, that they are sinners in need of cleansing, prodigals in need of coming home to the Father. Nevertheless, to be the world's salt and light is our call. And that call carries with it a promise: "Lo, I am with you always, to the close of the age." The One who calls is the One who is also present. In whatever form it comes, our call at its core is an invitation to be with Christ. This is why it is irresistible.

Index

111667